how to use

The Dynamics
of Motivation

James K. Van Fleet

Parker Publishing Company, Inc.   *West Nyack, N.Y.*

PRINTED IN THE UNITED STATES OF AMERICA
B&P

What the Dynamics
of Motivation
Will Do for You

It's long been said there are two main reasons why only 5 men out of every 100 attain some degree of financial success. One reason is said to be hard work; the other—knowledge.

But as important as these two factors might be and I know they're vital in any financial achievement—I don't see how they could possibly guarantee a man's success in today's hard-driving business world. By themselves, they're just not enough.

Today, your success or failure as an executive, as a member of the management team, will depend primarily on how well you can *motivate* the people who work for you—the people who carry out your orders.

Now then. Just what does this term *motivation* really mean, anyway? Well, to me at least, and I've made a study of it for twenty-five years, it means getting a man into that frame of mind where he'll want to do his utmost for me, and then—he'll do it.

In business or industry, isn't this what motivation should really mean? It should mean your ability to get your employee to work just as hard as you want him to work. It should mean your ability to inspire him to give you increased production or increased sales. And that increased production, or sales will mean an increased profit for you, the manager.

Unfortunately though, most executives have only a vague idea about how to motivate their employees to do their utmost for them. Oh, a lot of them have read psychology books, manuals on proper personnel management, trade journals about how to effectively control and lead their employees but the majority of them have failed to find the necessary inspiration they're looking for, or the proper guidance they need in these sources.

And not only that, *motivation,* both of the individual and of the group is a term that few people really understand. So most executives pass the buck along to the department in charge of industrial relations, personnel management, labor relations or whatever the name might happen to be in that particular company and try to wash their hands of the whole affair.

Or worse, they'll turn to the old-fashioned method of using threats and fear to control their employees. They'll try to increase production or sales by threatening the employee with either demotion or discharge if he fails to meet his sales or his production quota. And his fear will soon change to hate.

Nor is financial reward in itself enough. It, too, is old-fashioned if that's all you can offer to a man. If money were the only answer to increased sales or to increased production, then you could simply tell the man what his job is, pay him once a week or so—walk away, forget all about him, and go fishing. But will that method work? Hardly.

So here now is where this book, *How to Use the Dynamics of Motivation,* comes into the picture. It will give you the *eleven exact dynamic laws of motivation* for your guidelines to follow in dealing with your employees. There are exactly eleven—no more, no less. If there were twelve, the twelfth one would be to *put the first eleven into action and make them work.* If you'll follow these eleven dynamic laws of motivation, then you'll learn how to:

1. *Develop yourself so that you will be technically and professionally qualified and proficient in your work.*
2. *Know yourself and seek self-improvement.*
3. *Know your men and look out for their welfare.*
4. *Keep your men informed.*
5. *Insure that the task is understood, supervised, and accomplished.*

6. *Train your men as a team.*
7. *Make sound and timely decisions.*
8. *Develop a sense of responsibility in your subordinates.*
9. *Seek responsibility and take responsibility for your actions.*
10. *Always set the example.*
11. *Make every single man important.*

I'll also give you detailed methods of application which will show you how to put each one of these dynamic laws of motivation into practical effect in your daily activities.

Now then. Why is the proper motivation of your employee so important to you anyway? Well, I think that in the end you'll find that the most valuable asset your company has is not its physical plant, its real estate, or its machinery. It's the individual performance of each and every employee.

Individual performance. That's the most important measure of your company—no matter what its size. And that individual performance is completely dependent upon how well you've motivated that man to do his job.

So whether you supervise three people or three thousand, you'll find this book will give you those exact guidelines you need to follow in your use of the dynamic principles of motivation.

In short, it will show you how to use the dynamics of motivation in your supervision and in your management of your personnel so that you can make more money. Ever since the Phoenicians invented money several thousand years ago, it's been the primary aim of every man, hasn't it? This book will help you make more of it.

Contents

*Knowing your men and looking out for their welfare will motivate
them to have a much better feeling and attitude toward you and*

*Always set the example so your men can use you and your actions
to determine their own standards of conduct and efficiency . . . .
Your individual appearance and conduct must be such that they'll
bring forth from your subordinates respect and pride, and they'll
be motivated with a desire to meet your standards . . . . Always set
the standard for your entire organization by your outstanding performance of duty, and you'll motivate your employees to reach that*

You've Got to Know Your Business— and Stick to It!

Knowing your job and sticking to it will gain for you the respect and the confidence of your employees.

One of the biggest factors in the success of the Great Atlantic and Pacific Tea Company has always been said to be "sticking to the grocery business."

By concentrating on the sale of groceries and only groceries, they have gained the confidence of their customers. They have proven that they know their business.

And by knowing their business, they continue to *motivate* their customers to keep coming back year after year. How successful have they been in doing this? Well, they started in the middle 1800's and they're still going strong as the world's largest food retailer.

You can also gain the respect and the confidence of your own employees by knowing your business and then, by sticking to it. Don't try to know everything about everything. It just can't be done. Stick to your own business, not to someone else's.

One of the basic fundamentals of successful salesmanship is to *concentrate your attention on a single point and not to scatter*

1

your fire. The same principle applies here. Be an expert on your own job, not on everyone else's job. *Don't scatter your own fire.*

Your men will respect you and have confidence in you when you become an expert in your own field. So follow the example of the Great A&P. Learn your business, know it inside out—and stick to it.

> When you know your business—and stick to it—you'll also gain the willing obedience, the loyal cooperation, the full support of your employees.

When your employees see that you're not trying to bluff your way through, and that you really do know your business—then they'll trust your ability and your decisions.

Once you've gained their respect and their confidence, then you'll also be able to obtain their willing obedience, their loyal cooperation, and their full support.

But you've got to know your profession thoroughly. No one will follow you anywhere if they're smarter than you are about your own job. You've got to motivate them by knowing more than they do.

> Knowing your job and sticking to it will encourage your employees to work just as hard as you do.

Of course, the real goal of motivation of your employees is to get them to do their best for you all the time. To achieve that goal, you must be able to reach every man in your organization in such a way that each one of them will be inspired to give forth with his best efforts possible, every minute of the working day, in line with his own individual abilities. Knowing your own job and sticking to it will encourage your employees to do just that.

How It Works

About two thousand years ago, Horace, the celebrated Roman poet said, "I attend to the business of other people, having lost my own." And if you don't concentrate on your own affairs, the same thing can happen to you.

The real key to knowing your business—and sticking to it—is the ability to concentrate your attention on a single point and not to scatter your fire! Some of the oldest names in American business and industry have used this dynamic law of motivation as the first step in becoming successful.

For example, when you think of sewing machines, you automatically think of Singer; vacuum cleaners, Hoover; diamonds, Tiffany's; men's clothing, Brooks Brothers; groceries, the Great A&P; the Pride of Texas, Neiman-Marcus; soap, Procter and Gamble; the 5 and 10, Woolworth; automotive mass production, Ford. Every one of these great organizations, and many others, too, have become successful by knowing their business—and by sticking to it!

To help you know your business—and stick to it, I'm going to give you eight exact techniques which you can use to make this first dynamic law of motivation work for you. If you'll use these techniques meticulously in your daily contacts with your employees, you'll soon be able to inspire every one of them to give forth with his best efforts for you in his work.

First of all, I'd like to list these eight exact techniques of this first dynamic law of motivation so you'll have a better idea of just what we'll be aiming for in the rest of this section.

After that I'll take them up one at a time in more detail. I'll also give you some examples of how others have used them to become successful.

The Eight Keys for Application of the First Dynamic Law of Motivation

You've got to know your business—and stick to it.

1. *You must seek and gain a well-rounded education for your chosen profession.*
2. *Broaden your own professional and technical knowledge by making friends with those who are in associated or allied groups and professions.*

3. *Always look for opportunities to use your knowledge through the actual use and practice of the motivation of others to do your desires.*
4. *Keep up with current business and industrial developments and trends.*
5. *Build up a close association and friendship with those whom you know to be well qualified and capable in your own particular field.*
6. *You must know and understand the capabilities and the limitations of your own organization.*
7. *Always take advantage of every opportunity to prepare yourself for the next higher position of management within your organization.*
8. *Understand fully and apply properly the principles of sound management of your manpower, time, resources, and money.*

Discussion of the Eight Keys for Application of the First Dynamic Law of Motivation

1. You must seek and gain a well-rounded education for your chosen profession.

Always continue to improve yourself.

Don't stop studying just because you've graduated from school. You'll never live long enough to know everything there is to know about your chosen profession.

Continue to study, to read, and to research into every corner of your chosen occupation. And if you're now working, but you still want to improve yourself by other than your own reading at home in the evenings, then give some deep and serious thought to taking some correspondence courses or to attending some night schools.

Will it pay you dividends to continue your professional education and development? Can you motivate your own employees to a better performance by your own educational advancement?

Or perhaps even more important to all of us at times: *can you motivate the boss as well as your employees by improving yourself?* Well, I know this much for sure. Jim Taylor made it pay.

Jim Taylor makes it work.

At one time I was fortunate enough to visit the western part of North Carolina, better known as the *Land of the Sky.*

But its green mountains, clear lakes, and blue skies are not its only attractions. It also boasts of all kinds of textile mills, paper mills, plastic and rubber products factories, and many others. It abounds in industry, thanks mainly to its fresh, clear mountain streams.

A friend of mine, Jim Taylor, was the plant manager for the Waynesville, North Carolina branch of the Dayton Rubber Company when I first met him. But only a short year before that he'd been one of the general foremen in that same factory. How did he go up the ladder so fast in that short time? Well, let's see what Jim has to say about that himself.

"I always kept myself ready to take over my boss's job," he told me. "And during the time I was general foreman in the mill department, I also made it my business to learn what the main duties of the other general foremen and department heads were.

"I wasn't trying to run the other fellow's business but since my own department supplied everyone else with the raw materials to make the finished product, I had to know what was going on in their departments, too.

"Actually, I was broadening my own education and background so I'd be better able to understand the other foremen's problems. Well, as a result, I was pretty well informed about the overall operation of the entire plant. At least I could talk the language of every division we had.

"That extra knowledge paid off for me, for during that time, more than once the plant manager and the production superintendent had to go to Ohio on company business. And Tom always picked me to run the plant in their absence.

"About six months ago, Tom, our plant manager, got transferred to the main corporation offices up in Ohio. Harold, the production superintendent, took over Tom's job, and I became the production superintendent.

"Not long after that, Harold went to the Midwest to take over one of our plants in St. Louis, and they gave me the plant manager's spot here."

"What else did you do to prepare yourself for that manager's job, Jim?" I asked him. "I'm sure there was more to it than that, wasn't there?"

"Well, as I say, I've always tried to know as much about the whole business as I possibly could," Jim said. "I tried to learn my own job, my boss's job, and the jobs of each one of my men.

"But I did do a little more than that, too. As you probably know, I'm not a college graduate, so I was taking some courses down at Western Carolina on Wednesday nights and Saturday mornings. In fact I still do.

"The company knew I was taking some college courses, for they were paying for half of my tuition costs. I guess they must've felt that continuing my education was important to them as well as to me. And it must have been, or I'm sure that I wouldn't be managing one of their plants for them today. I've always done the best I knew how so I could be ready to take over when they were ready for me."

Pick your own method.

No matter how you do it, keep right on learning something new every day. The day you fail to do this has been a partially wasted day in your life.

Let me ask you this. How long do you think an incompetent doctor can keep his patients? Would you keep on going to a doctor who couldn't get you well? Of course not. At any rate, I don't think you would. I know I wouldn't.

Or what about a lawyer? Would you hire one to defend you who's never yet won his first case? I don't think so. The lawyer who can't win a case will not long be a lawyer.

So if you're going to be a doctor, you've got to be the smartest one in town. If you're a lawyer, you've got to be the best one around. This same idea holds true for any occupation or profession that you'd like to name.

2. Broaden your own professional and technical knowledge by making friends with those who are in associated or allied groups and professions.

Don't specialize too much.

If you're going to be a successful executive, then don't specialize too much. In other words, don't narrow your field of knowledge and understanding too far. If you'll make friends with others in associated fields, you can broaden your outlook and your viewpoint.

Too specialized an approach breeds technicians; a broad general viewpoint breeds executives and managers. I'm not trying to imply here that technicians aren't needed. They are. And so are managers and executives, only more so.

I'm only assuming that you're not interested in being only a technician since you're reading this book. I haven't met very many technicians who are at all interested in the motivation of others. But let me give you two examples here. Both are people I know well. One is a technician, the other an executive.

Meet the Technician.

The first of them, let's just call him Henry, is technically qualified and is highly proficient as a chemist—*but only as a chemist.* He's the typical absent-minded professor type. Shoes unshined, hair rumpled, no crease in his trousers, devoted to the technical aspects of his field—chemical engineering.

But Henry will always be a technician; that's what he evidently wants perhaps. He'll go no further than he is right now; I'm sure of that. You see, Henry will retire in two more years. He's 63 now.

Oh, don't misunderstand me. Henry's good. He knows his chemistry, but he couldn't motivate a mouse to eat cheese.

Meet the Executive—the Master Motivator.

The next man, Howard, is technically qualified, too. He's a chemical engineer, and he's one of the best. He's extremely proficient in his work, and he's kept right up-to-date by attending classes at the University. Experience has also added to his value with top management and with his company.

Howard is also professionally qualified and proficient. His shoes are shined; the crease is in his pants. His hair is combed; face always clean-shaven. His voice is soft but persuasive. His bearing that of a gentleman. Howard is the professional executive. He's the head of his department and headed on up the ladder, too. But Howard is far more than a technician.

You see, he learned early in this game of business competition that *technicians work only with things. Executives work with people.* And Howard knew that the main job of an executive is to use people to get those things done. Yes, Howard is the executive type. He's the professional, and he also knows his technical business about chemical engineering.

3. Always look for opportunities to use your knowledge through the actual use and practice of the motivation of others to do your desires.

Learn by doing.

The art of the motivation of others to do your will is acquired and developed only through actual practice, so you can gain the necessary experience. A man learns best by doing; it's the most reliable of all known teaching methods.

4. Keep up with current business and industrial developments and trends.

Don't limit your knowledge.

Don't limit yourself in this area to just your own particular field or profession, but make sure to keep a good eye posted on those vocations and professions that are closely allied and related to your own.

And not only that. Don't close your mind to another man's ideas just because he happens to be in a different profession.

You just might learn something worthwhile that you could use in your own.

5. Build up a close association and friendship with those whom you know to be well-qualified and capable in your own particular field.

Pride can lead to ignorance.

Don't be so proud that you can't learn something from another man. Observe others in action. See how they work. Study their actions closely so you can improve yourself. A long time ago Ralph Waldo Emerson said, "Everyman I meet is my superior in some way. In that, I learn of him." That statement is still just as true today as it was years and years ago.

If you want to learn, then ask!

One good way to learn all about your subordinates' jobs is to be honest with them and with yourself, too. You must be willing to learn from others, no matter what their position is or who they are.

If you're really smart, you'll simply own up to the fact that you just might not know everything that there is to know and then humbly ask your employees to help you out. *And they will, too.*

You see, you won't degrade yourself by asking your employees for their help, their opinions, or their advice. The lowest paid employee in your plant with the meanest job there is would like to let you know just how smart he is, how intelligent he really is, how much he actually knows. If you don't believe that, well, just ask him a question sometime. He'll tell you if you'll be courteous enough to listen to his answers.

If you want to be smart and rich, motivate your men by listening to them.

The smartest and, incidentally, the richest bosses don't consider it a crime that they should have to learn something from the men who work for them. So if you do want to keep on learning more about your own job, your own plant, your own department, your own employees, then ask them questions.

You'll really accomplish several things by this procedure of asking your employees questions. First of all, you'll often learn something of real value when you do ask a man for his opinion or his advice on a particular matter. Next, you'll motivate your own employees to think for themselves. Not only that, you'll motivate them to develop their own initiative, their own resourcefulness, and their own ingenuity. Do that, and they'll earn you more money.

6. You must know and understand the capabilities and the limitations of your own organization.

Don't be a stranger in your own plant.

The only way you'll ever find out the capabilities and the limitations of your own organization is to get out from behind that desk of yours. You must know what your plant is capable of producing, and then you must see that it is produced.

Don't let your salesmen oversell your production capacity, but don't ever let your plant under-produce what your salesmen have committed you to produce. You'll never motivate your customers to stay with you that way.

So circulate. Make frequent visits around your organization. Conduct periodic inspections of your subordinate supervisors. Check the work of your men. Supervise your supervisors; inspect your inspectors.

7. Always take advantage of every opportunity to prepare yourself for the next higher position of management within your organization.

Always be ready to move up.

You must train yourself so that you will always be ready to take over your superior's position at a moment's notice. If you don't do this, rest assured that someone else will. If you're not ready for your opportunity, you can be sure that someone else always will be.

There's no substitute for knowledge.

If you're going to be ready to jump into your boss's shoes, then you'll have to know your own individual profession—your own particular occupation—from the inside out. You must know it from the ground up. You simply have to know everything there is to know about it. There's absolutely no substitute for knowledge here.

If you're going to know your profession thoroughly, you must have a very specific knowledge of its most intimate and intricate details. If you're going to be successful in your management, in your executive position, you'll have to make it your business to know and to understand every step in the operation that's under your control.

Knowing just the big picture isn't enough.

I know it's often said that management ought to concern itself only with the big picture, and that executives shouldn't have to worry about the minor details. What I've just said might seem to contradict that or at least, it appears to do so on the surface.

But please notice this point if you will. I didn't say that you had to be able to perform all of the detailed work as well as the men who are being paid to take care of those intricate details. I said that you'd have to know and to understand every step in the operation that you control or that you're responsible for supervising.

There's a big difference between knowing and doing.

You see—here's the difference. Your men are being paid to do the exact details of their work. But you're being paid to see that they do it. Of course, you've got to know what they're supposed to do, but that doesn't mean that you yourself have to be the expert at doing it.

For example now, you might not be able to do some manual job quite as well as the man who's doing it—*but you've absolutely got to know what he's doing and why he's doing it!* Otherwise, you'd never be able to even begin to pick out any of his mistakes and correct him, would you?

And if you don't really know what a man's job is or what his exact duties are, how can you possibly expect to guide him or to motivate him in his daily work? If you don't know his job, if you don't know how important his work is to the team effort —you'll never be able to gain his respect and his confidence, will you?

Remember your primary mission is to motivate others to do the job.

I'd like to emphasize once more that you couldn't possibly be as good on a man's job as he is. Or at least, you shouldn't be. If you're as good as he is, then you're taking away from the importance of his job.

You're belittling a man if you imply that anyone could take over his job and do it as well as he can in just a short time with no background or experience whatsoever. Even the janitor would be insulted if you did that to him. It took me a long time to learn that idea. One of my men taught me that valuable lesson.

How Walter Brown looks at it.

One day I was watching Walter Brown work, and I marveled at the smoothness of his actions, the rhythmic, sure way in which he handled his raw materials and his machinery with his hands. "Walter," I said, "you absolutely amaze me. Why, I'd never in all the world be able to do that as well as you do."

Walter looked up at me from his bench and grinned. "Well, I should hope not," he said. "If you could do it as well as I do, then I might be out of a job.

"But you're forgetting something, aren't you?" he went on. "Remember, I'm supposed to be the expert around here with the tools and the machinery and with my hands. But you're supposed to be the expert with methods and people. Just because I'm a good man with machinery doesn't make me the expert when it comes to handling people, does it?

"So if you're the expert when it comes to dealing with people, then don't try to be an expert machinist, too. Can't do everything in this life, can we?

"But just as I'm supposed to know what your job is, you've got to know what mine is, too. That way everything works out real well for both of us, doesn't it?"

And he's right at that—isn't he?

Unless you know your business—your employees will lose confidence in you.

If you don't have the technical and the professional know-how it takes to hold down your job—if you show a lack of knowledge in any part of your work—your subordinates will soon lose confidence in your technical abilities.

And not only that, they'll soon lose complete confidence in you when it comes to your other abilities, too. You'll never be able to motivate them to do their best for you when you're trying to bluff your way along.

You've got to be motivated, too.

To motivate your employees to do their utmost for you, you'll have to exhibit personal diligence on the job yourself. Look at it this way. It's impossible for you to motivate your employees to do their best for you—if you are not motivated enough to also do your best for your boss.

Of course you might say, "Well, it's his job to motivate me. If I have to figure out ways to motivate my own people to do their best work for me, let him figure it out the same way."

If that's the way you feel about it, if that's the way you're looking at it, you're forgetting one extremely important point. You're on the management team, remember? You're an executive, a manager, a supervisor. You're supposed to be able to motivate yourself! Otherwise, this upward chain of motivation would never end. I mean—who would motivate your boss? And who motivates him? Who motivates the motivator?

The best motivators of employees are those people who are

themselves already self-motivated. They are hard-working people who are almost totally committed to, perhaps just short of being obsessed by, their work.

You can best motivate by your own example.

You can best motivate your own men by your own personal example. You yourself are the image of the company you work for. You represent the company to the men who work for you. So don't expect them to give their utmost to the company if you aren't giving your utmost to them. You can't motivate men on the production line if you're out on the golf greens.

And if you're not the boss yourself, I know this is one of the best ways in the world to put your boss on notice that you're really serious about this business of getting somewhere. You can bet he'll notice you if you'll put everything you've got into your job.

He'll have to notice you for there are so many people who put nothing into their jobs at all, but who want to take everything out. You know the kind I mean, I'm sure. The kind who think the company owes them a living just for showing up at work that morning.

There's no better way to motivate your boss into promoting you, into giving you that raise than to do such an outstandingly good job that he has to notice you. He has no other choice. And of course, if you're going to do such an excellent job that he'll remember you when the time comes for advancement, then you'd better keep yourself technically and professionally qualified and proficient, hadn't you?

Remember this dynamic law of motivation: *You've got to know your business—and stick to it!* And motivating your boss is just as much a part of the business as motivating your employees, especially when it's your own promotion that's at stake.

How Dave Smith works this technique of being ready.

A good friend of mine, Dave Smith, who works for the Springfield, Missouri Plant of the Lily-Tulip Cup Corporation, told me that his company felt this way about promotions and being prepared for the next job on up the line.

"Our personnel management people tell us this," he said. "Everyone in the plant is expected to be ready to jump right into his boss's shoes. And he'd better be able to do it, too. They're not kidding about that for one single minute, I can tell you for sure.

"If one of the department heads dies, gets sick, or quits, and we have to go outside the plant to get a replacement," he continued, "well, something's really wrong. Then we're just not doing our jobs properly. That's all there is to that. We just haven't prepared ourselves for that next higher position of responsibility. That's the way they look at it. They want to be able to promote from inside the plant, not from outside of it.

"In fact, they encourage us to keep up our education by going to night school, taking some correspondence courses, or whatever else we think might help improve our education and knowledge. And they put it down on our records. You know, continuing my education and keeping myself posted and up-to-date on my boss's job has really helped me out."

Dave ought to know. He started out 14 years ago for that company working on the assembly line in production. Today, he's their production superintendent, and right now he's next in line for the plant manager's job.

The plant manager? Where's he going? Oh, he's been preparing himself to step into one of the vice-president's jobs back in their main offices in Chicago. So you see, it really does pay to keep yourself technically and professionally qualified, both on your own job and in preparation to take over your boss's job, too.

Jack Hudson has this to say about it.

Jack Hudson with McDonnell's in St. Louis tells me that his company feels about the same way when it comes to promotions, advancement, and keeping yourself qualified.

"There's a mandatory retirement rule in our company," he told me. "If you're earning at least 15 thousand dollars a year, you've got to retire when you're 63. They won't even let you wait until you're 65.

"Of course, that's good," he went on. "That way, promotions are fast and our chances for advancement are good. My company makes regular estimates of its future requirements for executives and managers. For assignment to top management positions, they pick out the people as much as five years in advance.

"But let me tell you this," he said. "You really have to know the job of the guy above you if you want to go on up the ladder. It sure keeps you hopping. Why, when just one man retires, it can mean the promotion of 10 to 15 people.

"And if you're not ready—well, they just drop you right out of the picture. They go right on around you. We're still a young company, you know, and we're still growing even though we've made a big name for ourselves in just the last few years.

"But we haven't got time to wait around on people who aren't ready. We're aiming for the moon; the sky's the limit in our outfit."

8. Understand fully and apply properly the principles of sound management of your manpower, time, resources, and money.

Remember your goal in motivation.

After all, the goal of your motivation of your employees to do their utmost for you is your own profit and financial success, isn't it? So don't throw your profits out the back door faster than you can bring them in the front door by not knowing how to properly control your main factors of sound management.

Sound management usually has its foundation in the kitchen— not in the dining room.

A good friend of mine, Gary French, owned and managed an extremely successful restaurant for more than 25 years. Yet many people who ate there didn't even know that Gary owned the place. Why? Gary spent 95 percent of his time out in the kitchen.

When I asked him why he did this when he was the owner and could sit out in front wearing a clean white shirt, he said, "The waste in the dining room the customer is paying for. The waste in the kitchen I am paying for. So I'll stay in the kitchen. That's where my profits are."

You should do the same. In other words, go where you can best control your organization, no matter where that place is.

To Sum It All Up

You must be well-rounded in your profession, no matter how your knowledge about your field was gathered, whether by formal education, practical experience only, or both.

To be well-rounded means that you must have not only a broad and general knowledge of your profession but, in addition, you must also possess a specific knowledge of its most intimate and intricate details.

You must continue to seek out more information about your own field. To remain static is but to slide backward. You've got to know your own job, your subordinate's job, and your superior's job if you don't want to be left in the dust of your contemporaries.

If you know your business—and stick to it, you'll be able to gain the respect, the confidence, the willing obedience, the loyal cooperation, the full support of all of your employees. You'll be able to motivate them to do their utmost for you. And it's important to you to get their utmost from them. Any less is not enough. Stopping at third base adds no more to the score than striking out!

Recapitulation of the Eight Keys for Application of the First Dynamic Law of Motivation

1. *You must seek and gain a well-rounded education for your chosen profession.*
2. *Broaden your own professional and technical knowledge by making friends with those who are in associated or allied groups and professions.*

3. *Always look for opportunities to use your knowledge through the actual use and practice of the motivation of others to do your desires.*
4. *Keep up with current business and industrial developments and trends.*
5. *Build up a close association and friendship with those whom you know to be well-qualified and capable in your own particular field.*
6. *You must know and understand the capabilities and the limitations of your own organization.*
7. *Always take advantage of every opportunity to prepare yourself for the next higher position of management within your organization.*
8. *Understand fully and apply properly the principles of sound management of your manpower, time, resources, and money.*

If You Want to Improve—
Be Honest with Yourself

An honest and forthright evaluation of yourself will allow you to recognize your strengths and identify your weaknesses.

When you make an honest inventory of your good and bad points, recognize your strengths and admit your weaknesses, then you'll be able to take the first important step toward self-improvement.

Knowing yourself will allow you to recognize the basic fact that you don't have certain talents that others do have—but that you also have a lot they don't have.

Of course, one of the most important steps here is to find out what you're best suited for in the first place. One of the best things that can ever happen to a young person is for him to find out what profession or what vocation he's best suited for in life while he's still in school.

By taking an honest inventory, you'll be able to tell the difference between your limitations and your shortcomings.

If you're fortunate enough to do this early in your life, you're that much better off. You'll be able to save years and years of wasted time and effort. Too many of us confuse our limitations with our shortcomings, and there's so much difference between the two of them. The important point here is not to try and make yourself into something you don't have the God-given talent for in the first place. It only leads to disappointment, bitterness, and eventual frustration.

You'll be able to motivate others to do what you want them to do by setting the example for them to follow.

No one can hope to become successful in his motivation of others until he first knows his own capabilities and his own limitations, corrects those limitations, and becomes, in effect, the *master of himself*. And you cannot hope to master or motivate others until you are first the master of yourself.

How It Works

If you want to improve, it'll take much more than just wishful thinking. And it'll take a lot more than hard work, too; effort means nothing without results. Moreover, to improve yourself, you've got to be honest with yourself. You can't afford to be wrong here. Psychiatry is the only business where the customer is always wrong, and being honest with yourself is not psychiatry.

There are eight exact techniques you can use to make this dynamic law of motivation work for you. They represent a condensation of self-improvement methods which you can apply daily to motivate yourself, and by the same token, your employees. A lot of the enthusiasm and improvement of a self-motivated person just naturally has to rub off on those who work for him.

The Eight Keys for Application of the Second Dynamic Law of Motivation

If you want to improve—be honest with yourself.

1. *Analyze yourself and do it objectively and realistically.*
2. *Sincerely ask for the advice and the opinions of others who*

can help you to improve yourself and your own executive
qualities and abilities.

3. *Try to profit by the experiences of others.*
4. *Develop a deep and genuine interest in people. Learn to
   treat a man as a human being—not as an animal or a machine.*
5. *Master the art of effective writing and speaking.*
6. *Become friendly with members of your own profession and
   of allied professions who are already successful.*
7. *Develop your own philosophy of life as soon as you can
   while you're still young.*
8. *Never give up.*

Discussion of the Eight Keys for Application of the Second Dynamic Law of Motivation

1. Analyze yourself and do it objectively and realistically.

Analyze both your personal and your professional qualities.

You must honestly and forthrightly evaluate and inventory
yourself so you can recognize your own strengths and your own
weaknesses.

Here, I'm referring to the improvement of your technical and
your professional abilities just as much as I'm talking about improving your personal qualities and your character traits.

Both aspects are quite proper when we're concerned with
knowing yourself and seeking self-improvement. Always, always
strive for perfection, but never let it lead you to frustration.

Both of these areas, your personal qualities and your technical
and professional development, must be constantly improved if
you want to become completely successful in the art of motivating others to do what you want them to do.

But you can't even set out on a self-improvement program
unless you know and fully understand your own capabilities as
well as your own limitations. That is the only way you'll ever be

able to strengthen your good points and to get rid of your weak ones.

However, you must be self-motivated enough to want improvement for yourself. But you can't be wishy-washy about improving yourself and getting rid of your weak points. You've really got to have a lot of courage about it. You must certainly be the master of yourself before you can ever hope to master others by your motivation of them.

Take a long look in the mirror.

So if you're really serious about improving yourself, take a good long look at yourself in the mirror. Have courage when you do. Take a true inventory to find out your strong points and to isolate those weak ones. Then make the honest effort to overcome those weak ones. Improve on and strengthen those where you are already strong.

But please, be completely honest with yourself; take a complete and unbiased audit. To lie to yourself at a time like this will accomplish nothing for you at all.

Then continue to take this personal inventory at definite time intervals, weekly or monthly. And keep right on doing so for the rest of your life if you want to keep on improving yourself day by day.

Personally, I have to practice this idea of a personal inventory on a daily basis, and sometimes even on an hourly basis as a situation comes up or the occasion demands.

If I'd let my resentments pile up for a week, a month, or more, I'm afraid I'd never get an honest inventory completed. I'd be far too busy taking everyone else's inventory in those long intervals between.

It really does take a lot of courage.

Usually, with most people at any rate, it takes a lot of courage to apply this second dynamic law of motivation to their own lives. Oh, it's always so easy to see where the other fellow needs a lot of self-improvement, but it's oh-so-hard to see where you're in need of any changes.

What is courage anyway?

We've talked a lot about courage already. What is it anyway? It is one of your personal qualities, isn't it? Well, there are basically two kinds of courage: *moral and physical.*

We usually think of courage as being that attitude or that response of facing and dealing with any situation which is dangerous, difficult, or painful instead of trying to get out of it. It is that personal quality of being fearless and brave. That's what we usually think of when we talk of how brave or how courageous someone is. That's how we look at physical courage.

But there's another part of courage, too, and it's what we call *moral courage.* And moral courage can be a lot tougher to hang onto sometimes than is physical courage. Moral courage is when you have the courage of your convictions to do what you know to be right, no matter what the consequences might happen to be for you.

Physical courage is based on moral courage.

Physical courage has its source in moral courage. The two of them make up that mental state that well recognizes the fear of either physical danger or scathing criticism. But your courage allows you to go ahead in the face of that danger or that criticism, calmly, firmly, and serenely toward a definite goal with purpose and direction of action.

Courage is that calmness, that firmness, and that serenity of mind that will give you the ability to have control over your own emotions and over your own actions.

And that is the kind of courage that you will need to accept responsibility and to act the right way, to do the right thing, to say the right thing, in any kind of a situation, even though it might be threatening or dangerous or critical.

How the military looks at courage.

When the military services speak of courage, physical courage is usually thought of first and is always stressed. Medals and decorations in the service are based on physical acts of bravery.

But without fearless and strong moral courage for its base, physical bravery cannot long exist. *Physical bravery begins in the mind, not in the muscles.*

What is moral courage then?

Moral courage means that you will stand for what you believe to be right, even though you might be completely at odds with popular opinion and you might be risking disfavor, criticism, even condemnation.

When you have a strong moral courage, you will quickly and willingly admit your own errors and your own mistakes, but you will also enforce the decisions that you know are morally right, even at the risk of losing your popularity with your employees. But that kind of popularity is better lost anyway. It has no staying power.

Stand up and be counted.

You could say that moral courage is intellectual honesty or the willingness to stand up and be counted. One word of caution is in order here. Don't confuse moral courage with stubbornness or self-righteousness. They're really not the same at all. In fact, they're far removed from each other.

The development of a strong moral courage is an important factor in knowing yourself and seeking for your own self-improvement.

To develop and maintain both a strong physical and moral courage, practice these seven guidelines at all times.

1. *Study and understand your own reactions to fear.*

Always remember that fear is only an emotion, and that you must keep all of your emotions under control at all times if you want to motivate your men to do their utmost for you. You'll never be able to motivate them if you allow your emotions to come to the surface all the time.

2. *Keep and maintain an orderly and systematic thought process.*

Don't exaggerate physical dangers in your mind. Don't let your imagination run riot. Fear of the unknown is usually much worse than the real thing.

3. *Keep a calm, firm, and serene attitude.*

Once you've developed an orderly thought process and once you've gotten your emotions under control, then continue to control your fears by disciplining yourself in all of your actions to an attitude of calmness, firmness, and serenity.

4. *Force yourself to do the right thing, to do what is required of you in your particular position.*

If there are certain things that you have to do in your daily work that you actually fear or dread to do, then force yourself to do these undesirable things until you've reached the point where you no longer fear to do them. You'll know that you have complete control of yourself when you no longer fear these things.

5. *Stand for what you know to be right.*

Stand for what you know to be right even in the face of popular opinion. Have the courage of your convictions. Never compromise or prostitute your principles just because you are afraid of public criticism.

6. *Be ready to accept the blame if you're wrong.*

If you're wrong, have the courage to say so. Always be ready and willing to take the blame at all times if you did make the mistake. Accept the blame when you know full well that you are the one who is really at fault.

7. *Always remember that many times the only thing you really have to fear is fear itself.*

As I said just a few moments ago, it takes a lot of courage to apply this second dynamic law of motivation in your own life.

I, too, can so easily find fault with everyone else but myself. It's so easy to criticize others. Many times we try to justify our own mistakes by saying, "But just look at Harry! Gee, what I did isn't half as bad as what he did!" But two wrongs can never make a right, can they?

If you'll sincerely follow these seven guidelines for developing physical and moral courage and practice them daily, you'll soon see a big difference in yourself when it comes to both physical and moral courage.

And your employees will see the difference too. Now, let's get back to the first key or technique for application of this second dynamic law of motivation—analyzing yourself objectively and realistically.

Find out what you're best suited for.

Of course, one of the most important steps here is to find out what you're best suited for in the first place. Don't try to make yourself into something for which you have no inborn talents.

One of the best things that can ever happen to a young person is to find out what profession or vocation he's best suited for in life while he's still in school.

The ability to determine this early in life will save you a lot of wasted time, effort, and money. Part of the trouble is that too many of us do confuse our limitations with our shortcomings, and there's such a big difference between the two.

Don't drift.

So many of us seem to drift quite by accident into a job or a profession that isn't really to our liking at all. Then we're afraid to make the change to something else later on in our lives because of our many obligations.

But you know as well as I do that no one can be happy doing a job he doesn't like to do and isn't properly fitted for in the first place.

Limitations versus shortcomings.

We discussed limitations and shortcomings briefly a while ago, but it's extremely important that you get started off on the right foot in this business of motivation, so I want to talk about them just a little more.

Knowing yourself, many times begins with simply accepting the fact that you just don't have certain talents that others do have.

But those are your limitations. They are not your shortcomings. I know that every girl wants to become a movie actress or a television star; every boy dreams of being a pro ball player, but such dreams come true for only a very few.

The best thing that you can do is to take those talents that God gave to you in the first place and make the most of them. Maybe that's good advice for parents, too. It might keep them from forcing little Johnny to follow in father's footsteps, or from making little Sally do what mother never got around to doing.

Just take me for instance now . . .

My mother, for example, was absolutely convinced that I had all the makings of a great pianist within me somewhere. Either that, or she was trying to make me into what she herself had always wanted to be.

At any rate, my parents spent a good many dollars on my so-called musical education, and I spent many more hours practicing on an old upright piano that I hated with a passion.

And I do know this much about it too. I still can't play the thing.

2. Sincerely ask for the advice and the opinions of others who can help you to improve yourself and your own executive qualities and abilities.

When advice is given—listen.

Be sure that you listen when the advice you've asked for is given. Just remember which one of you is asking for help. Be certain to explore all possibilities to gain information for your continued improvement. A lot of good advice can come up to you from the actual working level, that is, if you're not too high and mighty to listen.

Lee Horne says this about asking for advice.

Lee is the sales manager for the Kendall Refining Corporation in Tulsa, Oklahoma, and here's what he told me about how he helps out younger executives in the organization when they come to him for advice.

"I have a lot of the junior management fellows come to me

for help and advice," Lee said. "I tell each one that I'd like to think his problem over for a couple of days before I make any concrete recommendations.

"During that time, I get out and talk to his own employees about his particular problem, and sure as anything, I'll always come up with an answer.

"And I always find out something else, too. Nine times out of ten, that same suggestion I got from the employee was also given to the fellow who came to me for help, but he wouldn't listen! Thought their employees couldn't possibly have the answer to such a weighty problem.

"When they come back to me and I give them the advice I've gotten from their own men, they look impressed and say, 'What a brilliant idea! Now why didn't I think of that?'

"Oh, they'll catch on to me one of these days. When they do, they'll have learned an extremely valuable lesson about where to get advice. I had to learn my lesson the same hard way."

3. Try to profit by the experiences of others.

Do some research of your own.

Study and search out the underlying causes for the failures, and also the successes, of other people, both past and present. Find out why they failed or why they succeeded. Then you ought to be able to avoid the mistakes of those people who have failed and to pattern your actions after those people who have been successful.

Ralph Leonard says this about failures.

"I've never learned a thing from my victories. The only time I ever learned anything was when I made a mistake and lost."

I don't know how many mistakes Ralph had to make to get where he is in the business world today, but he must have learned something along the way. Today he's the head of his own world-wide import-export company with headquarters in San Francisco.

4. Develop a deep and genuine interest in people. Learn to treat a man as a human being, not as an animal or a machine.

You've got to have the human touch.

If you want to be successful in motivating people to do their utmost for you, you'll have to gain early in life what is called the *human touch.*

If you're going to be a successful executive—a leader of men, the master motivator—you've simply got to know how to stimulate them to do your bidding. And you've got to lead your men, not push them, you know. Have you ever tried to push a piece of string? That's why you have to pull, not push.

You've got to like people to motivate them.

If you don't like people, if you can't develop a deep and genuinely sincere interest in them and in their problems, you'll never make a top-notch executive. You'll always be a loner, even when you're in the middle of a crowd.

Developing a sincere interest in people paid off for George Brown.

Having a deep and genuine interest in other people is one of the main reasons George Brown has been so successful in his huge variety store in Chicago.

When George was a young man working in his father's small dry-goods and notions store, he learned the value of placing the interest of his customers first.

Women especially liked to have George wait on them for he was always polite and painstaking with them and he always respected their desires.

Not only that, George had a lasting memory for names and faces. Of course, his memory was helped along by a small book in which he made notes about all his customers, their families, and their special likes and dislikes. This interest in other people has paid rich dividends for him.

"That's the biggest secret of salesmanship," George told me. "If you want to be a top-notch salesman, you've got to find out what the other fellow really wants, and then help him get it.

"And you can't find out what he really wants when you're talking about your own interests all the time. You've got to concentrate your attention on what he wants, not on what you want."

5. Master the art of effective writing and speaking.

Go straight to the point.

You must be able to say what you want to say clearly and concisely so that people will always understand you. Then they will know exactly what it is you want from them.

If they don't understand what it is that you want them to do, then how are you ever going to motivate them to work hard for you, to get the mission accomplished for you?

So go straight to the point. Say exactly what you want to say in as few words as possible. The fewer words you use, the less chance for error.

Improve your writing, too.

For some reason, it's hard for most of us to express ourselves clearly in writing. The best way to do this, at least for me, is to write exactly as I would talk face-to-face with another person.

Oh, I might dangle a participle now and then, or even split an infinitive occasionally, but at least most people know what I'm talking about. And Rudolf Flesch, the author of many books on modern-day English and grammar, says that splitting an infinitive or ending a sentence with a preposition isn't a capital offense anymore anyway. Bergen Evans, co-author of *A Dictionary of Contemporary American Usage* agrees with him. So who am I to argue?

In writing, too, it's best to come straight to the point. Don't freeze up just because you have a pen in your hand and a piece of paper on your desk in front of you. If people understand you when you talk, then you shouldn't have any trouble at all in expressing yourself on paper. That is, of course, if you'll just remember to *write as you talk.*

Learn at least the basic elements.

You must learn at least the basic fundamentals of good grammar, proper pronunciation, and correct spelling. But when it comes to vocabulary, be careful. Make sure that you broaden yours only for catching, not for pitching! Just fit your words as closely as possible to your exact meaning. If you're talking about dogs, then say dogs, not animals.

6. Become friendly with members of your own profession and of allied professions who are already successful.

Learn from successful people, not from failures.

I know I said a while ago that you learn from defeats rather than from victories. But my point here is this: The successful man has learned from his own failures. Henry Ford didn't succeed the first time nor did Thomas A. Edison. But they learned from their mistakes. The failure who is still a failure is the man who hasn't learned a thing from his experience. So why should you try to learn anything from him?

Yet so many people will try to do just that. Perhaps they feel the successful man is just too busy to be bothered with them. It could well be that the failure is overly anxious to talk to anyone who'll listen to him. The world is filled with almost-greats, and misery loves company, you know.

At any rate, don't pay any attention to the man who's a failure. Don't listen to him. In fact, avoid him. If you want to stop drinking or smoking, ask the people who have quit, not those who still indulge.

So learn from those people who are already successful. Ask them questions; ask them for help. You'll be complimenting a man's judgment and his intelligence when you ask him for advice. Show a real interest in him and in his answers when you do ask for such advice.

Just remember this. All people are primarily interested in

themselves, and I don't care how rich or successful they are. They'll love to tell you just how they became so rich and successful and just how important they really are.

Be sure that you subordinate your interests to theirs if you're really serious about learning something from them.

7. Develop your own philosophy of life as soon as you can while you're still young.

Fix a definite and concrete goal for yourself.

If you'll fix a definite and concrete goal in your mind, then you'll be able to have the proper attitude toward your chosen work or your selected profession, toward your life in general, and people in particular.

Always plan ahead and work toward your goal. Don't let yourself go stale. It's easy to have stars in your eyes when you're in your twenties and thirties. It's a lot harder in your forties and fifties.

As the old fellow said, "I feel just as young as I used to, but it takes a lot more effort." Keep that attitude, and you'll be in fine shape for the long haul.

The sooner you can develop your own philosophy about life, and the proper attitude toward other people, just that much sooner will you be able to fix your goal firmly in your mind.

Then you can devote all your time and attention toward attaining that goal. And naturally, you can look forward to being financially successful just that much sooner, too.

8. Never give up.

What is the eternal question?

What is the eternal question every honest and sincere man will ask himself every single day of the week? Here's what it is. "How can I improve my state in life? How can I better my present condition?"

That's the real question that haunts every *sincere* man when he starts to work every single morning. If it doesn't, then it means that he's given up the battle. *Never give up!*

Let me ask you something right now. Have you ever noticed how we here in America always root for the under-dog? We're always prone to praise the fellow who's fought his way up from the back-alleys and who's made a success of himself in this life, now aren't we? We're always proud of him and perhaps just a little jealous sometimes, too. Let me tell you about a man who fought his way back.

Dick M. finds his way back.

A close friend of mine, who I'll call Dick M. for the purposes of anonymity, fought his way back to the top after alcohol had knocked him deep into the gutter and into a state hospital for the mentally ill.

Dick had been a prominent attorney, and had been highly successful in the practice of corporation law. He had everything going his way: a beautiful wife, two fine children, a home in the fashionable suburban area of Kansas City. Dick had only one problem, alcohol. But let Dick tell you himself:

"I was all right until I had that first drink," Dick says. "Then after that I seemed to lose all control, and I'd keep right on drinking until I passed out completely. I'd never stop. I had blackouts of all kinds, car wrecks, woke up in back alleys, found myself a hundred miles away from home the morning after.

"My practice was going right out from under me. What big corporation is going to trust a lawyer who's drunk day and night? Finally, I had myself committed to the state hospital in the hope that I'd find the answer to my problem before I went completely insane.

"In the hospital I met a group of people who called themselves Alcoholics Anonymous. They'd stopped drinking by accepting the fact that they were completely powerless to control their overpowering obsession with alcohol by themselves.

"These people were staying sober and enjoying it. They used to come out to the hospital every Wednesday night and hold meetings there for those of us who were in the hospital because of our problems with alcohol. Some of them had been in the hospital themselves.

"Well, I don't want to drag this out, but they told me that if I'd stop blaming other people for my troubles, grow up and accept the fact that I also had some responsibilities in life, then maybe I'd have a chance again.

"One of the 12 suggested steps in the Alcoholics Anonymous program, the fourth one, in fact, recommends that we make a searching and fearless moral inventory of ourselves.

"Well, much as I hated to do that, I knew I had to do it. For the first time in my life I saw myself as I really was, and I realized how badly I needed a lot of self-improvement. So I went to work on myself for a change."

Did Dick succeed? Yes, he most certainly did. Today, he's back in practice and doing very well for himself. He personally practiced this dynamic law of motivation and motivated himself to take the proper action to correct and improve his own behavior.

Yes, it certainly will work. It worked for Dick and for about a half million other members of Alcoholics Anonymous who are living, walking proof that this dynamic law of self-motivation can really work if you want it to, and if you'll make it work. And you surely don't have to go as far as Dick went to find out, do you?

To Sum It All Up

Knowing yourself and making an honest evaluation and inventory of your strengths and weaknesses is half the battle, that's for sure, but it's only the first half.

To make it really worthwhile, you must take definite and active steps to improve yourself by getting rid of your weaknesses and by building up your strong points.

You'll have to develop the personal qualities of courage, bearing, knowledge, loyalty, enthusiasm, integrity, a sense of justice, and a host of others. You'll have to learn to set the example.

If you do take the proper action to improve yourself, you'll grow a mile taller in the eyes of your men. And just as important, you'll really impress your boss, too.

Recapitulation of the Eight Keys for Application of the Second Dynamic Law of Motivation

1. *Analyze yourself and do it objectively and realistically.*
2. *Sincerely ask for the advice and the opinions of others who can help you to improve yourself and your own executive qualities and abilities.*
3. *Try to profit by the experiences of others.*
4. *Develop a deep and genuine interest in people. Learn to treat a man as a human being, not as an animal or a machine.*
5. *Master the art of effective writing and speaking.*
6. *Become friendly with members of your own profession and of allied professions who are already successful.*
7. *Develop your own philosophy of life as soon as you can while you're still young.*
8. *Never give up.*

Know Your Men and Look Out for Their Welfare

Knowing your men and looking out for their welfare will motivate them to have a much better feeling and attitude toward you and your organization.

When your men know that you're sincerely concerned about their personal welfare, not only on the job, but also off it, they'll have a far better feeling toward you and a better overall attitude toward your entire organization. This positive attitude of theirs will most certainly be helpful to you in winning their willing obedience, their confidence and respect, their loyal cooperation, and their whole-hearted support.

You'll increase the working output of every person.

By knowing the requirements of your employees, by providing for their physical needs on the job, and by offering them the opportunity to satisfy their basic wants, you'll be able to increase the working output of each person in your organization.

Increased production means increased profit for you.

When you know your men and when you look out for their welfare, their attitude toward you will be positive. They'll want to help you. Their desire to help you succeed in your endeavors will increase each person's output.

An increased individual output means an improvement in the overall efficiency of your organization, the increased production of a quality item or an increase in its sales.

And increased production of a quality item or an increase in its sales means an increased profit for you.

How It Works

There are twelve exact techniques which you can use to make this dynamic law of motivation work for you. If you'll properly apply them daily to motivate your employees, you'll soon be able to reach every person in your organization in such a way that each individual will be inspired to give forth with his best efforts possible, every minute of the day, in line with his own individual capabilities.

This is not the last time you'll hear about looking out for the welfare of your men. It is one of the two primary responsibilities of the executive, the manager, the motivator. The other main responsibility is the accomplishment of the mission. These two must always be balanced properly if you want to motivate your men.

The Twelve Keys for Application of the Third Dynamic Law of Motivation

Know your men and look out for their welfare.

1. *See the members of your organization as much as possible and let them see you.*
2. *You must be able to call each one of your employees by name.*
3. *You must develop an intimate knowledge and understanding of your employees through these personal contacts with them.*
4. *Always be concerned about the personal living conditions of your employees if it affects their output on the job.*

5. *Give your personal attention to a man's pay and to his personal problems.*
6. *Protect the health of your men by providing them with good working conditions.*
7. *Actively support a safety program.*
8. *Know the status of your men's morale.*
9. *Administer justice impartially and swiftly.*
10. *Distribute equally and fairly both the privileges and the distasteful tasks.*
11. *Provide proper recreational facilities for your men.*
12. *Share their problems.*

Discussion of the Twelve Keys for Application of the Third Dynamic Law of Motivation

1. See the members of your organization as much as possible and let them see you.

Be friendly and approachable.

You must be friendly and approachable with your employees. But you'll never get to know them, and they'll never get to know you or understand you if you stay behind your desk all day long. You've got to find time to get out and circulate around. Let your employees see you.

Always be friendly with your people and show them that you really do appreciate them and their efforts for you. You don't have to be overly familiar with a man to show him that you sincerely appreciate his work. Nor do you have to be a back-slapper to be friendly with him.

Use the time clock method.

Jack Davis, who has his own electrical appliance wholesale house in Kansas City, Missouri, uses what he calls the "time clock method" to greet his employees every morning.

"It took them quite a while to get the idea that I wasn't just trying to check up on what time they came to work when I first started beating them into the place," Jack told me.

"When I first started, I used to stand right beside the time clock, and I soon found out that was no good. The best way is to pick your point somewhere along their route of entry to your place, but at some distance away from that time clock.

"But the important thing to get across to them is that you honestly do want to see them and to say 'Good morning!' to them. It really doesn't take them too long to get that idea.

"I'll say this though. Beating my own employees to work so I could say 'Hello' to them as they come in the door has sure helped their tardiness and absenteeism. The boss's presence seems to add a lot of motivation for them not to be late or absent!"

Good employer-employee relations are a must today.

Good employer-employee relations are an absolute must in industry today. The days of "treat 'em rough and tell 'em nothing!" are long gone. Even if you're hesitant to use first names with your employees, you still must be just as considerate and courteous with them as you are with your own customers.

Try the Sears Roebuck method.

At one time I worked for Sears and Roebuck, and I've never forgotten the good close relationships which existed, not only among employees, but also between employer and employee.

This positive attitude of friendly cooperation simply had to flow over into the employee-customer relationship, and I'm convinced that this has a lot to do with the success of Sears.

Whenever I bought something in the store, I was always given the same considerate and courteous treatment as would be given an *outside customer*, even though the clerk waiting on me knew full well that I was a fellow employee.

On more than one occasion, I was waited on by the store manager or his assistant. They also treated me with the fullest deference and respect, assisted me in every way possible to make my purchase, and then thanked me sincerely for buying at Sears! And they knew I worked there, too.

In fact, I've been treated more cordially at Sears as a fellow employee making a purchase in the very store where I worked than I've been at other times in stores where I was really a full-fledged, honest-to-goodness customer.

Don't call the man to your office.

Don't call your employees to your office to give them their orders and their instructions. You can probably afford to leave your desk more than you can afford to have them leave their jobs anyway.

And don't let pride get in your way. Get rid of that desk when you're giving your orders; it's too often a barrier between you and your employees. Go out and see them for a change; it will do both of you a lot of good.

Never issue direct orders.

And when you do go to your employee's place of work to give him his instructions, never issue direct orders if you can avoid it. Instead, disguise your instructions, your orders, and your directives in the form of suggestions and requests.

If your people do have any initiative and ingenuity, if they do have any "get-up and go" about them at all, you'll get a lot better and faster results this way than by giving out with direct orders or harsh commands.

Try the "What do you think?" approach.

Try the approach of "What do you think about this, Jack?" "What's your opinion on this, Joe?" "Would you be good enough to do this for me, Tom?" or "Would you please do it this way for me, Henry?"

I know you'll be deeply gratified at the reaction of your employees, especially if you've been calling them to your office and using the direct order, "*Do it!*" approach in the past.

Praise the man's work.

Always use this opportunity to praise a man's work. To walk around the plant just to be seen will not accomplish your purpose. It will not get the results you want, motivation of your employees to do a better job for you.

You must talk to each one. And as long as you're going to talk to your employee, always praise his good work. And be sure that you praise his good work quickly. The impact is lost if you wait too long.

Everybody likes a compliment. I do; don't you? You'll find that people really thrive and grow on your appreciation of their good work. If you praise your men in front of their fellow employees, it will raise the morale of all of them. And that you can't do in your office sitting behind your desk.

2. You must be able to call each one of your employees by name.

A man's name is the sweetest sound in all the world to him.

A man's name is the sweetest sound to him in all the English language. To use it can often work what seems like magic. But if you forget it or mispronounce it, you're headed for trouble.

As a good executive, you ought to know the first names of your men, you ought to know their backgrounds, and you should have as much information as you can get about their families, even though at first this might be very scanty.

But what man could help but like you if you can remember his name or, better yet, the name of his son or his daughter, or if you inquire sincerely about the health of his wife, Susie?

How Jim Wilkins does it now.

"Today I know every man in my plant by his first name," Jim Wilkins told me. And that really takes some doing for Jim is the president of Kimberly Music Industries, Inc., a corporation in Chicago employing nearly five hundred people.

"Oh, once in a while I miss," Jim said, "especially if he's real new, but not too often. I learned early that you've just got to know who's working for you, and who isn't, too!

"But it wasn't always that way, I'll tell you that for sure. Used to be, I never paid any attention at all to the faces of the men who worked in my plant. I knew the general foremen and the main department heads, and I figured that was enough.

"One day, I saw a group of men standing around in my place, apparently doing nothing. Well, I went up to them, asked them what they thought they were doing anyway, loafing on the job, and told them to get back to work.

"Told 'em I hadn't hired them just to stand around and do nothing, and that if they didn't get with it, I'd fire them. But they just laughed at me. And to make matters even worse, so did a lot of the other employees who were watching from the sidelines.

"When they didn't do what I told them to do, well, I hate to say so, but I really blew my stack. Of course, that just put the frosting on the cake. It only made a bad situation even worse.

"Come to find out they didn't even work for me. Oh, I guess you could say they did in a way, but not really. You see, they were employed by an electrical contractor I'd hired to do some wiring in the plant. They were just waiting for their own foreman to come back with some special instructions.

"Since then, I'll guarantee you I've kept everything in this place on a personal first-name basis. And it's really paid me dividends in employee cooperation and quality production.

Treat your people as human beings, not cattle.

If you do want to motivate your men to do what you want them to do, you'll have to treat them as human beings, not as cattle. There's a big difference between a *team* and a *herd*.

People want to be known by their names, not by their clock numbers, "Hey you!" or "Fellas."

3. You must develop an intimate knowledge and understanding of your employees through these personal contacts with them.

If you're going to make the honest effort to learn the names of all your employees, then let me recommend that you go even one step further.

Develop an intimate knowledge and a deeper understanding of them through these personal contacts you have with them in your plant.

Learn each employee's individual characteristics.

If you want to motivate your employees to do their best for you, you'll need to know their personal idiosyncrasies, their peculiar little quirks. Every effort that you can make to gain such information, and then to use it to your own advantage to motivate them, cannot help but improve your working relationship with your employees.

Use your personnel records to your own advantage.

Always use whatever available administrative records you keep to learn all you can about a man. Keep them current and up-to-date. Post pertinent data about the employee as you learn more about him. Unfortunately, most personnel records end the day a man goes to work.

How George Wheeler does it.

George is the production superintendent of the Berry Electronics Plant in Wichita, Kansas. "I keep a photograph album by department," he told me. "I devote one page to each man. On that page I keep his photograph, his name, the names of his wife and children, their pictures, too, if I can get them, and all the personal facts I've been able to gather about him. Where he lives, what his hobbies are, and so on.

"I make it a point to talk to at least five men in the morning when I make my rounds of the plant and five more in the afternoon. But before I start around the plant, I check my photograph file first.

"You see, I don't just talk to people at random. It might look as if I do, and of course, that's what I want. But you can bet that I've picked out my personal targets for the day's conversations well in advance. It keeps me from making a lot of stupid mistakes or hurting a lot of feelings."

4. Always be concerned about the personal living conditions of your employees if it affects their output on the job.

You must be concerned about this factor only so far as it could affect the efficiency of your employees in their work and in their output on the job for you.

There is, after all, a limit to how far you can motivate an individual who works for you. How a man lives and where he lives are in a sense none of your business as long as it does not affect his work for you.

Of course, if you're not paying him enough in the first place to live decently, then it becomes of paramount importance to you. But you must use your own good judgment in this matter.

5. Give your personal attention to a man's pay and to his personal problems.

Make sure that your men are paid the proper amount at the proper time.

Looking out for the welfare of your employees is one of the most important dynamic laws of motivation you can practice. You'll always need to keep it foremost in your mind.

One of the main things you can do in this area to help you motivate your men properly is to make sure that they are paid promptly, and that they're paid the proper amount for the work they've done.

Show a deep and sincere interest in their personal problems.

No human being lives who doesn't have some kind of a problem. And every person with a problem is always looking for an attentive and sympathetic ear.

There's no surer way of getting a firm grip on your people than by helping them solve their personal problems that are causing them so much concern.

Show an employee that you want to help him, and you'll have found the most simple and the least expensive way you'll ever find to build deep and lasting cordial relationships with your men.

Don't be overly familiar with them.

In your relationships with your employees, don't become overly familiar with them at any time. They don't expect this from you, and they don't want any part of that from you either. Many embarrassing situations can come up when you're overly familiar with your subordinates.

An employee will quickly and deeply resent you if you use a patronizing attitude and manner toward him. He doesn't like you to act that way, for he cannot treat you the same way in turn. Here—the door swings only one way.

Plan ahead for their needs.

Always think and plan ahead for the needs of your employees. Their desire to satisfy their basic needs and wants is the only reason for their behavior. Remember that a person works for you primarily because of the salary you pay him, but that alone is not enough. You've got to consider other aspects of his job, too.

Whether they give out with their best efforts for you in their work will depend a great deal on how well you can take care of those various needs and wants for them on the job.

6. Protect the health of your men by providing them with good working conditions.

Use common sense and good judgment, but don't baby them.

As far as the working conditions of your employees go, you ought to provide them with all the comforts and all the privileges that are both possible and practicable. But whatever you do, don't coddle them or treat them like babies. They don't

want that kind of treatment, and they don't expect it from you.
But they do expect to be treated as gentlemen.

Use the gentlemanly approach with all your employees.

I asked Lloyd Harrison, owner and publisher of the *Herald
Tribune,* a daily in Overland Park, Ohio, why he was so suc-
cessful in keeping 95 percent of his employees with his paper.
Here's about what he told me:

"Well, first of all, I pay them a decent salary," he said. "But
that alone isn't nearly enough. So I try to give them the best
working conditions possible, and of course, that's a major factor in my employee retention.

"But one of the most important reasons, I believe, is this,"
he went on. "I always treat every person who works for me as
a gentleman.

"I treat him with courtesy and respect and dignity. I don't
care who he is or what his job is, general foreman or night
janitor. He must be important to me in some way, or I wouldn't
have hired him in the first place.

"You see, I feel that being concerned about the welfare of
your men covers a lot more ground than just their salaries and
their working conditions. I feel you've got to add importance
and dignity to a man's job. Treating him like a gentleman is
one of the ways I use to do just that."

Be selfish about it.

If you neglect the health and the welfare of your employees,
your production will be adversely affected. To promote good
working conditions for your men is not just a sign of human
understanding and good will.

It is selfish on your part, for when you promote good working conditions for them you'll benefit in the long run. You'll benefit by the simple fact that you'll be able to make every man
in your plant as effective as possible in his work for you.

Good lighting and good ventilation are musts.

Good lighting will cut down on eye strain; it will help you
get rid of safety hazards. It will prevent costly accidents, im-

prove the quality of the workmanship, heighten the morale and esprit of your men, and increase the total quantity of your production.

Proper ventilation, good heating and cooling systems, and elimination of unwanted and unnecessary noise will all help to improve worker efficiency by getting rid of employee fatigue.

Fatigue breeds both accidents and incidents. Air conditioning doesn't cost in the long run. It pays. It more than pays for itself in the increased efficiency of your employees. And increased employee efficiency means increased profits for you.

Good housekeeping is needed.

Good housekeeping, plain old simple cleanliness, is an important morale factor. No one likes to work in a place where everything is filthy to the touch, where dirt and grime have been allowed to gather on the floors and windows and where the washrooms look like pig pens.

The standards of any organization can be quickly judged by the condition, the cleanliness, and the general appearance of the employees' washrooms.

Oil companies learned this fact a long time ago. They push their service station managers and owners to keep their rest rooms clean and sanitary and attractive for the public. It helps them attract new business and to hold the old.

Next time you take your car to the garage, take a look at its washroom. Don't look at the one the customers use. Take a tour through the one where the mechanics and the rest of the garage employees wash up. You'll be able to quickly tell just what kind of care your car's been getting there.

In the end then . . .

Whatever you do for your employees on the job, just remember that you must always consider their health and their personal welfare in their working conditions.

Keeping your employee in tiptop shape is selfish on your part anyway. The skilled employee who stays at home sick in bed with the cold he caught working in your plant is costing you time, money, and loss of quality production. And you'll be paying premium pay, overtime, to the man who's taking his place.

7. You must actively support a strong safety program.

You must set the personal example for them to follow in this area. If you take short cuts yourself that have inherent danger within them, then don't expect your men to do otherwise.

A good safety program can cut the costs of your insurance premiums in your organization. Accidents can be very costly to you in many ways.

8. Know the status of your men's morale.

You must know what the mental attitude of your employees is toward you and toward your organization. You can check on the status of their morale by your frequent informal visits and by your inspections of the plant, either formal or informal.

Ask questions of them and then make sure that you listen carefully to their answers. You must use every possible source of information that becomes available to you to find out how high or low their morale is, and even more important, *why*.

9. Administer justice impartially and swiftly.

Justice is more than punishment.

Most people think that justice means only punishment. *But justice also includes reward.* Therefore, you must administer justice, both punishment and reward, impartially and swiftly, without either fear or favor.

In your executive position, you'll no doubt have to render justice from time to time in such important matters as promotion and privilege, reprimand and criticism, reward or punishment.

Therefore, you'll need to be righteous, impartial, fair, and correct. You must learn to be honest, just, and fair in your treatment of all your employees. You'll need to avoid any discrimination and prejudice in your decisions and in your actions.

Your decisions will be the acid test of your fairness and of your own understanding of people and their behavior. Men will admire and accept a strict superior just as long as he is just and impartial in his treatment of all of them. In short, you'll have to treat everyone in exactly the same way.

Don't use the good-fellow approach.

If you try to use the good-fellow approach in your handling of your subordinates, you'll soon lose your firm grip of authority on them. It always takes a long time for any executive to build up his reputation for being honest and just and fair in his treatment of his employees.

Since it will take you such a long time to build up this solid reputation for being just and fair with your employees, don't destroy their confidence and their trust in you by some careless error or the slightest bit of injustice in your treatment of them.

You could easily destroy in a few moments what has taken you months or even years to establish and build up. Repetition builds reputation, in both directions.

You must be impartial and consistent.

To be just, you must be impartial and consistent in carrying out the duties of your executive position. You must render reward and administer punishment strictly upon the merits and the requirements of each individual case.

You cannot allow your personal anger or your private prejudice to creep into your decisions. You must carefully avoid any prejudice of race, creed, or color if you want to have the reputation of being honest and square and fair with all your employees.

I'm not going to delve into the subject of racial prejudice here one way or the other. I'll simply say this about that subject from a management or a motivation point of view.

If you hire your men without any regard at all for the color of their skins, then treat them the same way after you've hired them. And if you can't follow this principle, then you shouldn't have hired them in the first place.

10. Distribute equally and fairly both the privileges and the distasteful tasks.

Mix honey with the vinegar.

Always make sure that everyone gets an equal share of both the bitter and the sweet. If a favored few get all the privileges while certain others pull all the dirty details, you'll have plenty of trouble on your hands, and that's for sure.

Don't let your employees pull the wool over your eyes, but don't let just one of them get stuck with doing all the dirty work either.

11. Provide proper recreational facilities for your men.

Build the field.

Always provide proper recreational facilities if this is at all possible and practical for your organization. If there's a vacant lot going to waste that belongs to your outfit, then make some kind of recreational facility out of it. Make it into a baseball field or a softball field. Set up some horseshoe pits.

Organize the team.

Once you have the field set up, don't stop there. You're only half-through. Now organize and support a baseball or softball team.

And if you really want this kind of effort to be successful, then make sure the rest of your off-duty employees get out and support your team. No one likes to play to an empty house. Professionals don't like to; amateurs like it even less.

Organize a bowling league.

If your organization has the strength, then set up your own bowling league. It's a wonderful way for your men to let off steam and not get hurt in the process.

Take it from me. If you're on management's team, this is one time you'd better make sure to lose to labor.

How Richard Smith does it.

Dick Smith, owner of an aluminum boat factory in Minneapolis, a highly profitable business in the lake-dotted state of Minnesota, told me this: "I fixed up a field behind the plant," he said. "We're way out at the edge of the city and there's 40 empty acres behind our place. So we made a baseball diamond, a softball field, some tennis courts, and some horseshoe pits.

"Now I'm too old for baseball, softball, or tennis, but pitching horseshoes, why, that's right down my alley.

"And it's one of the best ways I've found for an employee who's mad at me for some little thing to 'get even with the boss.'

"I just let him beat me during the lunch hour in a plain old-fashioned game of horseshoes. Makes him feel a lot better, and it helps me for he works better when he goes back inside at one o'clock.

"Oh, I don't lose all the time. I like to win, too. I only lose when it's necessary!"

12. Share their problems.

Share the problems of a man's heart and he'll support you all the way.

If you want to better understand your men and to win their hearts and their willing support, then you must be willing to share their problems. You must offer to help them in any way that you can.

To be able to do this with sincerity will require you to *place more emphasis on their problems than upon your own.* You'll need to have an attitude of complete unselfishness to do it.

To be selfish up to a point in life is perhaps a good thing. You are the most important person in your life just as your employee is the most important person in his life.

But you'll never motivate him by telling him how important

you are. In fact, he must never find out that you're more important to yourself than he is to you. You see, you'll motivate him only when you let him know how important he is.

Not only is he more important than you are, at least as far as motivating him is concerned, he has certain other rights which you don't have.

You have an obligation to him which he doesn't have to you. Since you're his employer, and therefore, responsible for his welfare, you have the obligation to put his personal welfare above your own. And that's no easy trick to do.

The unselfish executive always thinks of his men first.

The selfish executive is the one who will provide for his own comfort and his own personal advancement *at the expense of his employees.*

To be an unselfish executive, you must always place the welfare of your employees above your own. You can never gain your ends at their expense. He who would be the greatest of all must first be the servant of all.

Now your subordinates will expect you to play your part properly according to your position. They'll not begrudge you your title, your position, your comfort, or your prerogatives, *just as long as you use them to promote their interests, and not at the expense of their welfare.*

Executive positions are positions of service to others.

This might come as a surprise to some. Positions of management, positions of high executive leadership in huge organizations, are always created to serve others, not just as a reward to the individual filling that high and honorable position. And I do say "honorable"—not "honored."

Many an employee might be surprised to find out that the president of his company is supposed to be the servant of both the employees and the stockholders. A lot of company presidents might be surprised to learn that, too. Some already realize it; others do not. Those who do will stay; those who do not will go.

To think of your management position or your executive spot as a place which offers you only reward and privileges is completely wrong. Certainly, privileges do go along with your high position, but so does the responsibility of serving others.

You can never use your executive position to practice your own peculiar and petty idiosyncrasies. Your management position was created solely to allow you to *fulfill your responsibility to your superiors by serving your subordinates.*

Promotion is much more than reward—it is opportunity for further service.

If you today are filling a quite high management position, you must realize that it is not just a reward for your past performance alone. It is a position for you to use your present proven abilities and to develop your future talents and potential for your organization.

Although it may well be that you do occupy your present high position in the organization because of your excellent past performance of duty, still it is not just a reward as such. People who look at promotion only as reward never make it to the very top.

You were paid for your efforts of yesterday, yesterday. Promotion is based upon future potential far more than it is upon past performance. Oh, of course, future potential is estimated upon past performance, true enough. It has to be.

But still, you didn't get promoted only because you did a decent job in the past. Lots of people did good jobs. You had to have something more on the ball for the company. Someone saw some future in you. So don't try to rest on yesterday's victories. You can't dry today's wash in yesterday's sun.

Be willing to share the rough spots.

To truly be an unselfish leader, a successful executive, a considerate manager, and to motivate your men to do their best for you, you must be *willing* to share the same hardships, the same discomforts, and the same dangers as they do.

Don't make the mistake of saying there are no dangers in

today's industrial plants. If you say that, you've never seen inside of a steel plant or a textile mill or a rubber factory. Modern
machinery is deadly and dangerous as well as efficient.

If you have an air-conditioned office, but your employees
must work in sweltering heat cooled only by ventilating fans,
then at least get out there with him and sweat with him side
by side once in a while.

That act alone will do a lot of good for both of you. It will
establish a bond of friendship you'll never find in any other way.
It'll help him mentally: he'll love you for it. And it will probably help you physically, too.

You need only remember one warning: *When the boss gets
involved in the work, he's no longer the boss!* So best not to get
in too deep; leave yourself an escape route.

Try Bert Wilson's way.

"I never go through the plant but that I stop and lend my
hand somewhere," Bert told me. Bert's system must be good.
He's the assistant plant manager for the Springfield, Missouri
branch of the United Rubber Company, soon to be promoted
and transferred to the corporation's main offices in Ohio.

"In a rubber plant, there's always a skid that has rubber stuck
to it. It's miserable to get it off and into the mill," he went on.
"So whenever I see a mill-man sweating and tugging away at
a stubborn skid of rubber, I stop and help him pull at it.

"Maybe it doesn't really help him very much, but we rub el-
bows and I get my hands dirty and we both part with a big
fat grin for each other. And that's what I stopped for anyway."

Pass along the credit—absorb the blame.

As long as we're on the subject of sharing, you must remember to share the credit for a job well done, too. If your organization is to be commended for outstanding work or for some
worthwhile achievement, then make sure to pass along the proper
credit to those who have made this accomplishment possible for
you.

You can never expect to gain the respect of your men if you

take the personal credit for all the good things your organization does, but you refuse to assume your fair share of the blame and the responsibility for its failures.

A good way to remember who gets credit for doing what, is this simple statement: *The boss is responsible for all his organization does or fails to do.*

To Sum It All Up

You've got to make an honest effort to observe your men, to become personally acquainted with them, and to recognize their individual differences if you want to better understand why they do the things they do.

By anticipating and providing for their needs, you'll be able to get their willing obedience, their confidence and respect, their loyal cooperation, and their full support.

If your men really feel that you're deeply concerned about their welfare, and that you're honestly placing their interests above your own, they'll have a much better attitude toward you and your entire organization. They'll be anxious to help you succeed.

Recapitulation of the Twelve Keys for Application of the Third Dynamic Law of Motivation

1. *See the members of your organization as much as possible and let them see you.*
2. *You must be able to call each one of your employees by name.*
3. *You must develop an intimate knowledge and understanding of your employees through these personal contacts with them.*
4. *Always be concerned about the personal living conditions of an employee if it affects his output on the job.*
5. *Give your personal attention to a man's pay and to his personal problems.*

6. *Protect the health of your men by providing them with good working conditions.*
7. *Actively support a safety program.*
8. *Know the status of your men's morale.*
9. *Administer justice impartially and swiftly.*
10. *Distribute equally and fairly both the privileges and the distasteful tasks.*
11. *Provide proper recreational facilities for your men.*
12. *Share their problems.*

Always Keep
Your Men Informed

Keeping your men informed will encourage their initiative and enthusiasm—their teamwork and morale.

If you want to be able to motivate your men to do their utmost for you, you must be sure to keep them well-informed about their progress.

Everyone wants to know exactly how well he has done. He also wants to know definitely what you expect from him. From the lowest worker in your plant on up to the boss himself, every single person appreciates a word of thanks and a pat on the back for a job well done.

If you keep your people informed about their individual progress, and if you'll let them know exactly where they stand with you, you'll encourage their initiative and enthusiasm; you'll improve their teamwork and enhance their morale.

The well-informed employee is a more effective employee.

The man who knows the overall situation, who knows exactly what his job is, and who knows what you honestly think of him

and his work is a far more effective employee than the one who
does not.

The well-informed employee will always have a much better
attitude toward his superiors and the organization as a whole.
He can better understand just exactly what is expected from
him when he has been shown the objectives of the entire organization. A complete understanding of these objectives will help
him to establish his own goals and to then adjust his own behavior to reach those goals.

> *Keeping your employees informed will gain for you their respect,
> their confidence, their willing obedience, loyal cooperation, and
> full support.*

The individual employee and the group as a whole will appreciate your recognition and thanks for a job well done, for a
mission properly accomplished.

Through the proper application of an awards and incentive
program and the timely use of an effective information program,
you can favorably influence the morale, the esprit, the discipline,
and the individual proficiency of your employees.

When you know exactly what you want from your men, and
when they know exactly what you want from them, this mutual
understanding will gain their respect, their confidence, their willing obedience, and their full support.

> *Keeping your employees well-informed will eliminate rumors.*

It is usually the unknown that your employees will fear the
most. By keeping them well-informed, you'll be able to do away
with most idle rumors. When you do away with unfounded
rumors and idle gossip, you'll automatically reduce many of the
potential or actual unsatisfactory conditions that could cause
friction, dissatisfaction, frustration, and fear among your employees.

How It Works

"Why don't they let me know what's going on!" "Why don't
they tell me what they want?" "Why is it always hurry up and

wait!" "Why don't they make up their minds what they want?"

Have you ever heard comments like these before? I'm sure you have. So have I, many times. During World War II, when I was still stationed here in the United States, I'd read the headlines and I'd think, "I'd like to be right there and get the straight truth of it all." But when I got there, and when I was right in the thick of it in Europe, I'd still have to read the *Stars and Stripes* to find out where I was and what my own outfit had been doing!

Communication—the ability to transmit your orders and your commands, your wishes and your desires, down to the lowest working level—is one of the biggest headaches of a top-level executive.

But a lot of the problems can be corrected if you'll just use the eight specific techniques I'm going to give you. They'll make this dynamic law of motivation work for you.

If you'll properly apply them daily to motivate your employees, to keep them constantly informed, you'll soon be able to reach every man in your organization in such a way that each one will want to do his for you. And that's the purpose of the dynamic laws of motivation: to get your men to do their very best for you.

Eight Keys for Application of the Fourth Dynamic Law of Motivation

Always keep your men informed.

1. *Praise the successes of your men and your own organization to build up their morale and esprit so you can motivate them to do their best for you.*
2. *Explain to your principal subordinates why any specific task must be done, and exactly how you propose to do it.*
3. *Make sure by frequent supervisory visits that your subordinate supervisors are passing down the necessary information and the required orders to their men.*
4. *Always keep your principal subordinate supervisors informed of any of your plans for future operations.*

5. *Pass on all information to your men about rival companies and competitive products.*
6. *Be especially alert to detect the spread of false rumors. Stop rumors by replacing them with the truth.*
7. *Keep your men informed about current legislation and laws which could affect them, or any changes you propose to make in company policies.*
8. *Be sure a man knows what his job is, what his exact duties are, and who his immediate superior is.*

Discussion of the Eight Keys for Application of the Fourth Dynamic Law of Motivation

1. Praise the successes of your men and your own organization to build up their morale and esprit so you can motivate them to do their best for you.

If you like a man's work, tell him so.

"I never realized how important this was until I started losing some of my key men to big corporations," George Barnes told me. George has his own small oil company (small in comparison with corporations) in Little Rock, Arkansas.

"I figured that I paid my people better than the average big employer, and I thought money was enough. It didn't occur to me that a man wants to hear you say 'Thanks!' once in a while, too. I thought getting paid was enough.

"Now I know that everyone wants to hear just exactly how well he has done. From the lowest worker in my place right on up to the top, everyone appreciates a word of thanks and a pat on the back for a job well done. And you know something? I appreciate hearing it from my own men, too."

George is so right. If you like a man's work, you've got to tell him so. You must be able to arouse enthusiasm in your men by your motivation of them. And one of the best ways to do this, if not the best, in fact, is to show your appreciation for his work and to offer him encouragement and praise in his job.

Make his job important.

A good way of praising a man is to build up the value of his work. Tell him how essential his job is to your organization and how important he himself is to you.

Most people really need to think that their jobs are the most important ones in the plant, that their positions have a real status. So give that status to their positions. Most of your employees will need to feel essential to you and your efforts before they'll ever start clicking for you.

Praise the right man.

Another point for you to remember is to make sure that the right man gets the credit for the job that has been done. And that's doubly important to keep in mind if you, management, ever try to steal the credit that really belongs to one of the people who work for you.

Do that, and you'll completely destroy a man's initiative and his willingness to do something for you ever again. You'll never get that person to assume any more responsibility. He's no longer an asset to you; he's now a distinct liability.

You can get a double benefit.

If you'll give a man honest and fair recognition for his efforts, you'll find you're going to get a double benefit out of it. First of all, the man will get public recognition and reward for a job well done. Secondly, you'll win his loyal cooperation, willing obedience, and full support for the future. And that is one of your goals in using the dynamics of motivation, isn't it?

Never criticize anyone.

By the same token, there's nothing in the world that will so kill the ambitions of a man to do a good job as criticism from his superiors. Never, never criticize anyone. Warranted or unwarranted, criticism will do nothing positive for you at all. It'll only destroy all your other efforts to motivate a man to do his best for you. Let Harry Summers tell you how criticism nearly destroyed him.

How Harry Summers did it then.

Harry Summers, the production superintendent for the Allegheny Steel Corporation, Natrona Heights, Pennsylvania, always used to criticize his men in front of their fellow workers. He'd verbally cut them to ribbons about the quality of their work. It was bad enough for him to criticize a man, but when he failed to give that man the courtesy of privacy, he was doubling the penalty.

"I really used to lambast them," Harry told me. "And I really thought I was a terrific foreman when I did it. Rough and tough, that was me. Chew them up into little pieces and spit 'em right out on the floor in front of every worker close by. And they all watched and listened, you can bet that.

"Then like the fool I was, I couldn't figure out why the quality of our product kept right on going down-hill, and none of the men seemed to care at all. Absenteeism was sky-high, production was running about 85 percent, inspection and quality control was turning back 20 percent of that, and I could see my job flying right out the window.

"That's when you showed me how wrong I was, Jim. Just as you told me: When you criticize another man, he just automatically goes on the defensive, and all you end up with is a loud argument with both of you yelling at each other. Neither side gains a thing and the man's work gets worse instead of better. Then you came along, and brother, am I glad!"

How Harry Summers does it now.

"Here's what I do now," Harry went on. "When one of my men hasn't done as well as I know he should have done on a certain job, when the quality of his work is slipping, or when he just needs a plain old-fashioned pep talk, I ask him to drop into my office.

"First of all, I get him comfortable with a cup of coffee. Then I chase the secretary out so there'll be just us two in complete privacy. But before I ever come to the point, we talk about a lot of other things first. I still remember what you said about *praise first, last, and always. Suggest in between.*

"First we have some small talk. I ask him about his wife, family, how's the boy getting along in the Army, that sort of thing. When I finally get to the business at hand, I've got him softened up pretty well. By then he's ready for some help and advice. Here's just about what I say to him:

" 'John, you know I'm sort of disappointed in your showing in this. I don't think I've misjudged you, but it just might be I've overestimated your abilities to do this job. You see, John, I felt that you could do it a little better than what you did.

" 'To tell you the truth, John, I feel you've sort of let me down in this. But what's even more important yet is the fact that actually you've let yourself down. You've evidently become satisfied with getting only ordinary average results when we both know you're capable of doing a much better job.'

"It doesn't take many sessions like that before a guy gets right back on the ball," Harry went on. "In fact, Jim, if it takes more than one, I really do a double-take and wonder if it isn't about time for that man to look somewhere else for a job.

"But that's only happened to me once or twice since you came along. The thing is, a man appreciates my doing it this way. It sort of brings him up short and makes him take another look at himself without getting hurt in the process.

"And I haven't chewed him out, I haven't cussed him, I haven't made a fool out of him, or myself, for that matter, in front of all the other employees.

"And our production is right back up where it ought to be. Our quality control department can't find enough bad stuff to even keep their inspectors busy. They just can't find anything to turn back anymore."

Be hearty in your approbation and lavish in your praise.

Give a man a reason and an incentive to work hard for you by praising him. Always be hearty in your approbation and lavish in your praise of him. I could repeat that sentence on every page of this book, and still not say it too many times.

Always be hearty in your approbation and lavish in your praise.

Let me quickly point out here that if you do praise every little thing your employees do, then your praise possibly could lose its real meaning and true value. If medals for bravery were to be given out at random in the service, they would soon become completely worthless.

But even so, it would be better to make the mistake of praising too much than not enough or to criticize. And it will never hurt to use the magic words *Please* and *Thank You* all the time when you're dealing with your employees, or anyone else, for that matter.

2. Explain to your principal subordinates why any specific task must be done, and exactly how you propose to do it.

Praising a man isn't enough.

"Just praising a man isn't enough to get the job done," Mark Evans told me. Mark is the personnel manager for the Denver Power and Light Company in Denver, Colorado. "Just praising a man isn't enough to motivate him to do an outstanding job for you. If that were true, there wouldn't be any need for employment people like me. No amount of motivation will stimulate a man to do a job he's not qualified to do.

"However, if the man's qualified, then you can motivate him to do his best for you. Now each one of them will want to know just exactly what you expect from him. He'll want to know why something is being done, and he'll want you to show him how to do it."

Mark is right. If you will keep your employees well-informed on these aspects, it will help to encourage initiative on their part. It will improve their teamwork. They'll get along together much better.

Mark is also right in this respect. No amount of praise will motivate a man to do a job for which he's not qualified in the first place. That's why employment agencies will never go out of business, right?

Praise a man by giving him more responsibility.

One of the best ways to work this second technique for your own benefit, and yet praise a man at the same time, is to delegate even more responsibility to him.

Always give him the responsibility for the exact details of his own work. If you keep your hand mixed up in all the minutia of his job, you'll discourage your employees, for in a way, you'll actually be competing with them yourself.

Don't try to do it all yourself.

If you do try to do everything yourself, you'll soon completely destroy a man's initiative and his ingenuity. Sooner or later, the more capable individuals will quit and leave your organization, leaving you with only those who are perfectly content to sit back and watch you do all the work that they're getting paid to do.

To prevent this from happening to you, give the man a specific job to do; let him know what is required of him on that job as far as the details go, and then supervise him to see that he does what he's actually getting paid to do.

Give the man the Big Picture.

Keeping a man well-informed covers a much bigger area than just his own individual job and the details of his work. Keeping a man informed will require you to keep him posted on the activities of your whole organization. You should bring your people up-to-date all the time on new developments. Let them know well in advance whenever any changes are contemplated.

As members of your team, they're entitled to know what's going on. Give them enough information about conditions and events in your company and in the industry itself so they can see themselves and their own work in the proper perspective.

Keeping a man informed will raise his individual morale. Do that and you'll automatically raise the esprit of your whole organization.

The person who knows the situation and who knows where he

stands with you will be much more effective in his work for you
than the man who has to guess in the dark all the time.

3. Make sure by frequent supervisory visits that your subordinate supervisors are passing down the necessary information and the required orders to their men.

Issuing the order isn't enough.

Basically speaking, you could say there are three phases to
any order. Most people don't realize this. Many think all you have
to do is just issue an order. Some do know that it has to be
formulated before it's ever issued. But few realize that *no order is ever complete without the supervisory phase.*

The three parts of an order, then, are its formulation, its issuance, and its supervision. You must supervise to make sure that
your orders are reaching clear down to the working level, not
stagnating at some intermediate level in-between.

4. Always keep your principal subordinate supervisors informed of any of your plans for future operations.

Do this, and you'll cut out rumors.

When rumors fly around about expansion of the organization,
men are not too worried about losing their jobs. But when they
feel there's a possibility of cutting down on the operation or a
consolidation of various departments, they do worry about the
future. They definitely worry about losing their jobs. And the
more they worry about this problem, the worse becomes the quality of their work.

5. Pass on all information to your men about rival companies and competitive products.

Competition builds enthusiasm.

Here it's important for them to realize how vital it is for your
company to beat out all competition. If quality and price are

about equal, then you've got to emphasize the importance to them of the delivery and service factors to your customer.

At any rate, your men must understand how important outside competition is to their jobs and to their own future. The business graveyard is full of companies and their employees who underestimated their competitors. A competitor might be hard to live with, but he'd be a lot harder to live without. Competition motivates people to do their best. It always brings progress.

6. Be especially alert to detect the spread of false rumors. Stop rumors by replacing them with the truth.

Stop rumors before they start.

Always tell your employees the truth, and you'll eliminate 99 percent of your rumors. But if one does get started, there's only one sure way to stop it. That's by replacing it with the straight facts. Simply tell your men the unvarnished truth, and that's that. Truth will last much longer than a lie. Tell your men the truth and you never have to remember what you said.

7. Keep your men informed about current legislation and laws which could affect them, or any changes you propose to make in company policies.

A man's primary concern is himself.

Your men will be primarily concerned about those laws and those policies which could affect their pay, their privileges, their promotions, or any other of their benefits.

A man is mainly concerned with those changes which will affect his pocketbook. His wallet is still one of the closest things to a man's heart.

If you can, always keep them advised of the reasons behind the decisions you make that are going to affect them. They're not especially interested in your other decisions just as long as those decisions have no direct bearing on them and on their personal welfare.

They might be curious but not especially concerned or deeply interested. Each man's primary concern is always himself.

The well-informed person has a much better attitude.

"I used to think that what I did and what the company did was none of the employee's business," Jim Moore told me. Jim has his own nation-wide trucking firm with headquarters in one of the livestock capitols of the Midwest, Sioux City, Iowa.

"But I found out that if I'd let the fellows know what was going on company-wide, they had a much better attitude toward their dispatchers, their division chiefs, and toward me, too. Now we publish our own monthly news-letter for them, and we always include personal items about a man and his family as well as company news. Makes one big family out of the outfit, and we like it that way."

Jim is so right. Once the employee understands the big picture, he can then fix his own goals in his mind, and he can adjust his own work to reach those individual goals.

He'll work much better for you when he knows that his job is required and that you need him. So let him know that he is important to you and that his efforts are appreciated. Be hearty in your approbation and lavish in your praise.

8. Be sure a man knows what his job is, what his exact duties are, and who his immediate superior is.

A man can have only one direct superior.

Many industrial plants today make sure that each man knows what his exact job is. They also furnish the man with a complete job description so he'll know what his exact duties are.

Then they violate the third aspect, for they can never decide for sure who his immediate superior is. And no man can have two masters. It is impossible to serve both of them. He cannot be loyal to both.

Unless you make sure that each man has only one immediate superior, and that your chain of supervision is followed to the letter, you'll never develop a sense of loyalty in your employees. You'll have only widespread confusion.

Loyalty is a must if you want your employees to be motivated to do their best for you. It's also a personal quality you'll need to develop. Just as you expect loyalty from your own subordinates, they'll expect loyalty from you.

Loyalty is based upon a well-informed group of employees.

Unless you keep your men well-informed, you're asking them for blind loyalty. This will not work. Oh, after they've worked for you a while, and after you've proved to them that you're dependable, trustworthy, and loyal to them, they'll give you their loyalty without much question. But at first you'll have to earn it.

Loyalty is your desire to give faithful and willing support and service to both your superiors and your subordinates, in spite of your own personal feelings in the matter.

You must give unswerving loyalty to your superiors, to your subordinates, and to your organization if you want to become successful in your motivation of others. Your every act must show your personal loyalty to your organization. If you can't do that, then you ought to quit and go to work somewhere else.

Loyalty goes in both directions.

"I used to think loyalty was only for employees," said Lloyd Stark, a general foreman in the Autolite plant in Cleveland, Ohio. "I figured they owed me their loyalty, but I didn't realize I had to earn it. And I didn't think I owed them a thing. When the chips were down, they wouldn't stick up for me, and I lost my job. I learned the hard way.

"Now I know that loyalty is a door that swings both ways. It's like a stone thrown up into the air; it goes both up and down. If you want your men to stick up for you when the going gets rough, then you've got to defend them from unwarranted criticism and punishment from above. You've got to stand up for them. I do that now."

If you want to develop loyalty, follow these 9 guidelines.

1. *Always know who your superior is and who his superior is.*

You're entitled to know who your boss is, and you must also know who his boss is. By the same token, your men must know that you're their boss. Every man is entitled to know who his immediate superior is.

If your men know who their boss is, they'll always know exactly who has the authority to give them proper orders and who is stepping beyond the lines of his authority.

Knowing who the boss is will keep people from trying to pass the buck to someone else.

2. *Cooperate and work in harmony with your associates as a member of the team to develop your organization loyalty.*

3. *Be quick to defend—and always defend—your subordinates from all mistreatment and abuse.*

You are to protect your men from excessive or unwarranted punishment or abuse from your superiors. You should not try to protect them from punishment or reprimand which is deserved.

4. *Never show the slightest hint of disagreement with the orders of your superiors in front of your men.*

If you feel that you must question the actions and the orders of your superior, take the matter up with him in private. Don't do it in front of your men.

5. *Never criticize your superiors.*

Questioning your superior's actions is one thing; criticism of his actions is another. Don't criticize him, even to yourself. If you do, you'll never be able to keep your feelings toward him from coming to the surface and creeping into your work. You can't develop loyalty by criticism.

You must whole-heartedly support your superior's decisions, no matter what your own personal feelings are. Criticizing the boss is just another way of passing the buck upstairs.

6. *Do every duty assigned to you to the best of your ability.*

7. *Never discuss the personal problems of your men with others.*

Never violate the confidence your men have placed in you. Don't gossip; don't be a rumor monger. It's your job to squelch rumors, not to spread them.

8. *Stand up for your superiors, your subordinates, your associates, and your whole organization when any have been unjustly accused.*

9. *Always be extremely discreet in discussing your organization's activities outside the organization.*

Never talk about the problems, the activities, or the methods of management outside the walls of your own organization. Treat such matters as confidential or privileged unless you've been told otherwise.

To Sum It All Up

Everyone wants to know exactly what is expected of him. He also wants to know how well he has done. If you keep your men informed, you'll find this will encourage their initiative, it will improve their teamwork, and it will enhance their morale.

The man who knows the situation and who knows what is expected from him will do a far better job than the one who does not. It is always the unknown that your men will fear the most. Eliminate that fear, and you've gone a long way toward improving the overall efficiency of your organization.

Each individual and the entire group will appreciate your recognition of their efforts when a job has been especially well done. By the proper use of an awards and incentive program, and by the effective use of a well-planned public information program, you'll be able to favorably influence the individual morale and the organizational esprit. Improved efficiency and increased profits will be your end result.

Recapitulation of the Eight Keys for Application of the Fourth Dynamic Law of Motivation

1. *Praise the successes of your men and your own organization to build up their morale and esprit so you can motivate them to do their best for you.*
2. *Explain to your principal subordinates why any specific*

task must be done, and exactly how you propose to do it.

3. *Make sure by frequent supervisory visits that your subordinate supervisors are passing down the necessary information and the required orders to their men.*

4. *Always keep your principal subordinate supervisors informed of any of your plans for future operations.*

5. *Pass on all information to your men about rival companies and competitive products.*

6. *Be especially alert to detect the spread of false rumors. Stop rumors by replacing them with the truth.*

7. *Keep your men informed about current legislation and laws which could affect them, or any changes you propose to make in company policies.*

8. *Be sure a man knows what his job is, what his exact duties are, and who his immediate superior is.*

Make Sure The Task Is Understood, Supervised, and Accomplished

Your men will be motivated to work much more effectively for you when they know exactly what their job is and when they know exactly what you want them to do.

Your men will want to do a better job for you, if you'll tell them exactly what their job is, exactly what you want done, and precisely what results you expect from them. Many times a man's failure to do a good job comes from his lack of understanding of what you want from him. You must tell him what you expect and when you expect it.

Your men will respond much more quickly to orders which are concise, clear, and easy to understand.

You'll get much faster results from your men if your orders are simple, concise, and straight to the point. On the other hand, you can easily cause confusion if you overstate the order or instruction by giving too many details. Tell them what you want and when you want it, but not how to do it, if you want to get the best results from your men.

You'll be able to decentralize your work much more effectively so you can use your supervisory personnel to the utmost.

Your employees like to know that you are available for advice and counsel if and when you are needed. However, they always resent oversupervision and harassment. Always emphasize skill, not rules, and you'll cut your supervisory requirements to the minimum.

When your men know exactly what you want and precisely what their job is, then your foremen and your supervisors can be used to help them do their jobs.

Proper supervision *helps* a man do his job. Improper supervision *forces* him to do it. The test of a foreman or a supervisor, then, is not how good he is at bossing, but how *little* bossing he has to do to get the job done because of the training of his men and the organization of their work.

Emphasize results, not methods, in your orders, and you'll develop individual initiative and ingenuity in your men.

To motivate your men to do their best for you, use mission-type orders. A mission-type order tells a man what you want done, when you want it done, but it doesn't tell him how to do it. It opens the door wide for your men so they can use their imagination, their initiative, and their ingenuity in their jobs for you. It can lead to new methods and new methods can lead to more profits.

Making sure the task is understood, supervised, and accomplished will eliminate confusion and increase your profits.

Making sure each man knows his precise job and his exact duties will eliminate overlapping of work and duplication of effort. It will get ride of confusion and misunderstanding. When you make sure you have only one man doing one job, you'll increase your profits.

The Way to Make It Work for You

The properly motivated employee is industry's most valuable asset. But even the greatest asset will become a liability if it's improperly used.

Your employees must be *motivated for total performance* before they'll efficiently and willingly perform their assigned tasks.

Today, you see and hear a lot about *Zero Defects*. It's the striving of both business and industry, and also, the armed forces, to achieve the best possible results. But you'll never achieve your goal of *Zero Defects* until you've motivated your people for *total performance*.

One of the best ways to do this is through the use of the fifth dynamic law of motivation: making sure that the task is understood, supervised, and accomplished. And to make this dynamic law work, I'll give you twelve exact techniques which you can use. If you'll use them every day, you'll be able to develop your employees' initiative, imagination, and ingenuity to the utmost. You'll motivate them to total performance. Only then can you shoot for your goal of *Zero Defects*.

The Twelve Keys for Application of the Fifth Dynamic Law of Motivation

Make sure the task is understood, supervised, and accomplished.

1. *Make sure that the order you're going to give is needed before you give it.*
2. *Learn how to make a proper estimate of the situation.*
3. *Develop the ability to issue clear and concise, complete and correct, positive orders.*
4. *Always use your established supervisory or management chain of authority when you issue your orders.*
5. *Always encourage your subordinates to seek immediate clarification of any point in your orders they do not fully understand.*

6. *Oral orders should always be repeated back to you.*
7. *Supervise the execution of your orders.*
8. *Never use your established supervisory or management chain of authority when you personally supervise the execution of your orders.*
9. *Vary your supervisory routine during your inspections.*
10. *Always exercise thought and care in the supervision of your men.*
11. *Give your own personal assistance to your subordinates when it is requried.*
12. *A lack of orders does not relieve you from the responsibility of taking the necessary action.*

Discussion of the Twelve Keys for Application of the Fifth Dynamic Law of Motivation

1. Make sure that the order you're going to give is needed before you give it.

If you're the boss, your men already know it.

You don't need to issue an order just to prove that you're the boss. If you're in charge, your men know that fact already. You don't need to emphasize it. This will happen once in a while when a foreman or a supervisor is relatively new and wants to prove himself or occasionally when an executive becomes power-mad. Young second lieutenants and lance-corporals are most often accused of this failure in the services. But with experience and age usually comes understanding.

When you do issue an order, issue it in a firm and decisive manner which will show that you expect strict compliance and immediate action.

Never issue an order you can't enforce.

One of the secrets of good leadership and successful motivation of your men is to get complete and absolute obedience to every order that you issue.

At first this sounds hard to do, but really it's quite simple. Just do this: *Never issue an order that you cannot enforce.* Here's what Charlie Frost, a production foreman for the Royal McBee Typewriter Corporation, a Division of Litton Industries in Springfield, Missouri, has to say about it.

"One of the biggest stumbling blocks I had when I first became a production foreman was to get the men to follow my orders," Charlie told me. "But I was doing a couple of things the wrong way.

"First of all, I was giving a man an order to do something he couldn't possibly do in the time I gave him. Not only that, I didn't even check to see if he knew how to do the job or not. As a result, things were always fouled up on my assembly line, and my production was far below the normal quota.

"Here's the way I do it now. First I ask a man if he can do a certain thing for me. If he says 'Yes,' then I tell him to please go ahead and do it that way for me. If he says 'No,' I ask him why not and he tells me. Then I ask him what he can do and when he tells me, I ask him to do that. Either way I win."

2. Learn how to make a proper estimate of the situation.

You can't issue a proper order unless you know the situation.

Learning how to make a proper estimate of the situation is an absolute must before you ever issue an order. This step has to precede any order if you want that order to be effective.

Once you've decided on your course of action or your solution from your estimate of the situation, then you can *organize* your forces to do the job. Next, you can *deputize* by issuing your order through the chain of supervision that is available to you. And finally, you must *supervise* to make sure that your orders are being carried out to the letter.

Most executives and most managers do quite well until this last step of an order, *supervision*. Then they fall flat on their faces in this aspect of their management and motivation of their men, primarily because they don't know how to enforce their orders.

3. Develop the ability to issue clear and concise, complete and correct, positive orders.

Your ability to issue a proper and complete order will come only through study, review, and practical application. Only after long and careful training will you be able to achieve perfection in receiving, interpreting, obeying, and passing down orders to your subordinates.

Use mission-type orders to develop initiative in your men.

Your subordinate supervisors will develop their initiative when you give them work to do without telling them exactly how to do it. They'll be forced to use their imagination and ingenuity to develop specific techniques to accomplish the tasks you've given them. This is a *mission-type order*.

If you do use mission-type orders, and in the long run you'll have to if you want your organization to expand and progress profitably, then you must take certain definite steps to make sure that the task is understood, supervised, and accomplished.

What is a mission-type order and how does it work?

Exactly what is a mission-type order then? Simply said, *a mission-type order tells a man what you want done, but it doesn't tell him how to do it.*

A mission-type order states what your desired results are, but it doesn't tell a man what methods he must use to get those results for you. It emphasizes skill, not rules.

When you use mission-type orders, you open the door wide for your employee to use his initiative, his imagination, and his ingenuity to solve the problem you've handed him.

Why use mission-type orders?

Mission-type orders are a must if you want to get the maximum results from your organization. This is especially true in large corporations where the organization and the operation tend to become so complex and so widespread geographically that control has to be decentralized to get the job done.

Making sure that the task is understood, supervised, and accomplished is one of the keys to successful decentralization in big corporations that have branch industrial plants or branch retail stores scattered throughout the country. To accomplish their mission, they have to use mission-type orders.

Decentralize responsibility and you must decentralize authority.

The more decentralized the responsibility, the more must the authority to carry out that responsibility be given to your junior executives and your subordinate supervisors. Now don't think of this as passing the buck.

Giving a man the responsibility to complete a certain task or to do a certain job for you isn't passing the buck to him at all. If you're his boss, you still retain the overall responsibility for the accomplishment of the primary mission. That's yours, not his. Remember this though. Mission-type orders and decentralization of authority and responsibility all go together.

What Henry Wilson says about decentralization.

Henry Wilson, the local plant manager in Des Moines, Iowa, for DeWitt-Newton, Inc., builders of prefabricated homes, tells me that his company today is one of the leading proponents for decentralization and for using mission-type orders.

"They weren't always that way," he told me. "However, they've finally realized that unless they do decentralize to the extent of giving the local plant manager the responsibility and the authority to run things where he is, they just weren't going to grow any more. They'd reached the limits of their expansion. So now, they've changed completely. Their attitude is the opposite of what it used to be.

"Today, they believe in getting the local man to make those on-the-spot decisions," he said. "Now everyone in the plant, from my receptionist at the front desk to my shipping clerk at the back door, knows that I'm it. They know I'm solely responsible for running things here in Des Moines and for getting the job done.

"And they know they're working for me," he went on. "They know that what they do right here on the job has a direct effect on them and on me, too. And those effects are immediate, right now. They don't have to wait to get an answer from some main office or from some executive who's a thousand miles or more away. They know they can get a decision right on the spot from me. And that helps us to get the job done."

The higher the level, the broader the scope of the order.

The higher the level in the chain that is issuing the order, then the broader must be the scope and the overall mission that is given out.

There's a world of difference between Henry Wilson, a plant manager hundreds of miles away from his head office, and Charlie Frost, a production foreman in a factory where his boss is only a few feet away.

However, mission-type orders tend to make managers at all levels of supervision use initiative, resourcefulness, and imagination to get the job done. Each one is comparatively free in his choice of solutions to get the job done, free to accomplish the assigned mission just as long as he stays within the limits of his previously defined boundaries and policies.

Take George Dwyer for example.

George Dwyer, the local store manager in Omaha, Nebraska, for Fairfax Fashions, a prominent mid-west chain of ladies' clothing stores, told me this about his company's policies and way of thinking.

"When I first came out here to the Omaha branch," he said, "I could only spend up to 25 hundred dollars without first getting approval from our Chicago office.

"Since then, our head management has changed their minds and their ideas about how to run the branch stores. They've decentralized authority and responsibility all over the place. Now I can stock up to 25 thousand dollars worth of merchandise without having to get their OK first. If I still had to go into the main office before I committed our funds, I'd be getting my fall fashions in the spring!"

What mission-type orders will do for you.

If you've never used mission-type orders before, you're going to be in for an extremely pleasant surprise. Use them and you'll give your organization a flexibility you've never known before.

This will be especially true if you've been used to running a one-man-show sort of an organization. Mission-type orders are designed to bring out the best in your employees. They'll have to use their initiative, their imagination, and their ingenuity, or make way for those who can.

The structure and function of a mission-type order.

Let me describe a mission-type order in some detail for you so you can see exactly how it will work for you. First of all, it has three basic parts or three fundamental elements: *the mission, the limiting points, and the resources available.*

1. *The mission.*

A mission-type order must say clearly and concisely just exactly what is wanted by the person issuing the order. The order must state the exact objective that is to be reached, the precise results that you expect. In other words, *what is the mission to be accomplished? What is it that you want done?*

2. *The limiting points.*

The limiting points or the control factors must be pointed out in your order. That is to say, to what extent can your subordinate go in his methods to carry out your order, to accomplish your mission. *What exact limitations, if any, have you placed on him?*

A good rule of thumb to follow here is to *balance the welfare of the men against the accomplishment of the mission.* Do that, and you'll not have many problems or questions with what limitations to place on your subordinate.

3. *The resources available.*

Your order must say exactly and clearly what resources will be made available by you to your subordinate to accomplish your mission for you.

Be specific. Spell out in exact and definite terms the manpower, the time, the materials, and the facilities that you're going to give him to do the job for you.

Not only must you do this, you must also give him a clear-cut indication as to whether he can expect any outside help or support to complete the mission should the need came up.

What a mission-type order will not do for you.

The one thing, and the only one, that a mission-type order will not do for you is this: *It will not tell your subordinate how to do the job.* The how of it must be left up to him. The moment you tell him how to do the job you no longer have a mission-type order. You've taken away his flexibility completely. He can't use his ingenuity, his initiative, or his good judgment to resolve your problem for you.

If you don't use mission-type orders, you don't need human beings to do your work for you at all; all you need are the machines.

In the final analysis . . .

Mission-type orders will do this much for you, if nothing more: They'll *force* your subordinate leaders to make their own decisions and to figure out their own plans of action.

They'll bring out the initiative, the ingenuity, the imagination, and the resourcefulness of your subordinate supervisiors. Any subordinate who isn't stimulated to do a better job for you working under mission-type orders isn't worth his pay to you at all.

The use of mission-type orders is one of the most effective ways of weeding out rapidly the inefficient and incompetent subordinates in your organization before they become a burden to you. If you have young executives in your organization who can't handle this kind of an order, get rid of them. Replace them with those who can.

4. Always use your established supervisory or management chain of authority when you issue an order.

Only in emergency . . .

Never by-pass this chain of authority except in the case of an actual emergency. Then make sure that an emergency actually exists before you do. If you do, let those you've by-passed with your order know about it as quickly as you can.

Don't manufacture or dream up emergencies or high pressure situations. In short, don't push the panic button before there's an actual panic. You'll probably create one if you do.

Save your adrenalin until you need it.

Amazingly though, some people actually live from crisis to crisis. They can't be happy, or at least so they think, unless they're working in a state of constant panic or emergency, no matter whether it's real or imaginary. Usually it's imaginary.

Take John for example.

John, an army colonel I once knew, couldn't function properly unless he was working in some sort of a constant crisis. He used to work himself into an absolute frenzy over nothing. If the General sneezed, Colonel John caught a cold.

If he'd been able to produce under such circumstances, perhaps his actions might have been partially justifiable, but the fact of the matter is, he couldn't. And neither could the poor men who worked for him.

John ended up with peptic ulcers and a cardiac flutter and all without any real reason. But the poor fellow had never learned to take things in stride; he'd never learned to relax and take it easy.

If you burn up all your energy in imaginary crises, you'll never have enough adrenalin left for the real thing when it does come along. So save yourself so you can go full tilt when you really have to.

5. Always encourage your subordinates to seek immediate clarification of any point in your orders they do not fully understand.

If your subordinates don't ask you to clear up any doubtful points for them, don't just assume that everything is clearly understood by them just because they've asked no questions.

You must question them to make sure there's no possibility of doubt or misunderstanding about exactly what it is that you want done.

Find out the reason for disobedience before you take action.

Ambiguity, vagueness, and incompleteness of orders are more often than not the reasons for disobedience and honest mistakes or failures to obey your orders than any other cause.

Once in a while, you'll find a person who'll maliciously and wilfully disobey your orders, but this kind is out of the ordinary. Now an honest violation of your orders is one thing; malicious violation of them is quite another. Malicious disobedience must be dealt with promptly and summarily.

The *words* in your order tell what has to be done. The *wording* of it can influence the spirit in which your men will carry it out.

6. Oral orders should always be repeated back to you.

If you fail to require this of your men, it can often result in misunderstanding of what you actually want done. If your order is misinterpreted, your mission cannot possibly be accomplished.

7. Supervise the execution of your orders.

An order without supervision is not an order.

No order is ever considered complete unless your supervision is included. You must be firm but fair in your supervision. Always insist that your orders be carried out to the last minute detail.

Whenever possible, you should have your immediate administrative and technical assistants visit your subordinates to aid them in any way that they can. Make sure they offer assistance. Don't let them interfere with your operation.

8. Never use your established supervisory or management chain of authority when you personally supervise the execution of your orders.

Issuance of your order is one thing; supervision of it is quite another.

When you organize and deputize in the issuance of your orders, you always use your established supervisory or management chain of authority. When you supervise, you *never use that same supervisory chain of authority.*

In your supervision, always by-pass this chain of authority you used to issue your orders so you can *inspect and supervise at the lowest working level.* You yourself must do it. You have no other way to make sure that your orders and your instructions have actually gotten down to that working level where the job is to physically be done.

How Major Fowler does it.

Major Robert Fowler gave me an example of how he personally supervises the execution of his orders. Here's what Bob told me:

"Any military commander can issue an order," he said. "That's easy enough to do. As a battalion commander, it's so easy for me to say to my company commanders, 'Tomorrow every soldier in this battalion will carry a raincoat in his pack.'

"When I issue this order I use my leadership chain of authority, my company commanders. I always issue my orders and my directives through that chain of leadership. That's a must. But I never supervise through it. And that's also a must.

"Let's suppose the next day I want to check and see if my orders have been carried out. Should I ask the company commanders? I know their answers already, don't I? It's 'Yes sir!' of course. But how can I know that they know? I can't. So I can't supervise through my leadership chain of authority.

"If I really want to find out, I'll have to by-pass this chain of leadership, and personally check each soldier myself. But I simply don't have the time to look in the packs of a thousand men. I'll have to devise a different system.

"Here's how I do it. I go to a company and I ask the company commander to fall his company in. Then when they're standing there in formation, I have every man take his raincoat out of his pack and put it on. Then I can see for myself. And that doesn't take long at all to do that.

"There's no reliable substitute for this method of supervision if I really want to make sure the job's been done. I've yet to find another system that will take the place of this method of personal supervision and inspection."

Use a spot-check system.

What about the time element in your own case? I can hear you saying now, "But I can't possibly check every single person; I just don't have that much time in the day. And I can't line them up in a military formation either."

True, I agree. You might never be able to check your operation the way a military commander can check his men for raincoats.

But if a 100 percent check can't be used, then use a percentage or a spot check. Over a period of time this system will give you a 100 percent check of your operation. It just takes longer to get it done, that's all. And I'll show you a spot system in the very next technique that you can use quite well, I'm sure.

9. Vary your supervisory routine during your inspections.

Use the six-step supervisory inspection system.

1. *Allocate a certain amount of time each day for your supervisory inspections.*
Always inspect some phase of your operation every day.

You'll soon find that Monday mornings and Friday afternoons are the danger periods of the working week. (That's assuming, of course, that you're on a five day week, 40 hour schedule.) They're the let-down periods. So bear down on your inspections during these two critical periods.

2. *Review your inspection points before you inspect, not after.*

For example, the afternoon before pick out several specific points of interest or trouble spots for your next day's inspection. I recommend that you select no less than three, but not more than eight points of primary or major interest.

By changing these points daily, you'll soon cover your entire operation.

3. *When you inspect, inspect only your selected points of interest.*

Carefully go over your selected points of interest the afternoon before your inspection begins so you will know everything there is to know about those points, *but only those points.*

Be an expert only on the points you're going to cover during that one particular inspection. *Don't inspect anything else! Never try to be the expert on everything on any one single day.*

This detailed study you make before you inspect will refresh your memory. It will clear up any foggy points or any of the minute details for your next day's inspection. Use this system and you'll always look like an absolute expert in your field.

4. *To inspect is to emphasize.*

Emphasize your selected points in your supervisory inspection, not the points your subordinates are trying to select and emphasize to you. Remember who is inspecting and who is being inspected.

Only when you emphasize your selected points will you appear to be the expert. The moment you allow your attention to be drawn away by your subordinate supervisor to the place he's trying to lead you, you'll at once risk exposing your ignorance and lack of knowledge.

You must retain command of the situation if you always

want to appear to be the expert. Time, experience, and countless inspections will make you one.

5. *When you inspect, always by-pass your chain of authority.*

This is an absolute must. No other kind of inspection is ever satisfactory. Your subordinate leaders can and should go with you on your inspections, but don't question them. *Question their subordinates!* Remember the raincoat in the pack.

6. *When you inspect, listen.*

Don't talk except to ask questions. You are not inspecting to give out information; you are inspecting to get information. Not only that, you're not inspecting to show others how smart you are. They already know you're smart, or you wouldn't have your job. You must inspect to find out how smart they are. So ask questions, questions, and more questions.

10. Always exercise thought and care in the supervision of your men.

Don't over-supervise, and yet you dare not under-supervise!

Over-supervision will kill your men's initiative and cause resentment toward you. Over-supervision is really not supervision at all. It's only harassment.

Under-supervision will not get the job done for you either. You'll simply have to find the happy medium in your own case. How much supervision will depend upon both you and your employees. Some require very little; others take much more.

When you supervise, don't criticize.

A wise supervisor will not criticize. He'll suggest logical and constructive methods for improvement. *It is so easy to find things that are wrong. It's so much harder to find the best way to make them right.*

11. Give your own personal assistance to your subordinates when it is required.

When the boss gets involved in the work, he's no longer the boss.

If it's really necessary for you to pitch in and help to get the job done, then do so. Don't be afraid to get your hands dirty *once in a while.* Your men will think a lot more of you for helping out *when it's really needed, when the going gets rough.*

But such occasions should be rare. Something's wrong with your operation if your personal help is needed too often. Although it's wise to pitch in sometimes for the purposes of morale, be sure to remember this: *When the boss gets involved in the work he's no longer the boss!*

12. A lack of orders does not relieve you from the responsibility of taking the necessary action.

You are responsible.

You are responsible for all your organization does or fails to do. So always keep a complete picture of the situation in your mind so you can take the proper action in your superior's absence. Even if you have no specific orders to cover a certain situation, you'll be expected to take some appropriate action.

To Sum It All Up

To motivate your men to work more effectively for you, you must make sure that the task is understood, supervised, and accomplished. You must give clear and concise orders. You must make sure that your orders are understood. Then you must supervise to make sure that they are promptly and properly carried out.

The wise executive will decentralize his operation so that his orders and his directives can be carried out more readily. Failure to make good use of your subordinates will prevent your effective use of decentralization. By the same token, failure to decentralize will prevent the proper utilization of your subordinates.

Your men will respond more quickly to orders which are easily understood by them and which at the same time allow them to use their initiative and to develop their ingenuity. Use mission-type orders for the best possible results in your organization.

Recapitulation of the Twelve Keys for Application of the Fifth Dynamic Law of Motivation

1. *Make sure that the order you're going to give is needed before you give it.*
2. *Learn how to make a proper estimate of the situation.*
3. *Develop the ability to issue clear and concise, complete and correct, positive orders.*
4. *Always use your established supervisory or management chain of authority when you issue an order.*
5. *Always encourage your subordinates to seek immediate clarification of any point in your orders they do not fully understand.*
6. *Oral orders should always be repeated back to you.*
7. *Supervise the execution of your orders.*
8. *Never use your established supervisory or management chain of authority when you personally supervise the execution of your orders.*
9. *Vary your supervisory routine during your inspections.*
10. *Always exercise thought and care in the supervision of your men.*
11. *Give your personal assistance to your subordinates when it is required.*
12. *A lack of orders does not relieve you from the responsibility of taking the necessary action.*

Train Your Men
As a Team

When you train your men as a team, you'll give each one a sense of being needed and wanted and a feeling that he "belongs where he is."

One of the strongest psychological drives in a man is his desire to belong, to have identification with a certain group. Give him that identification he needs, and you'll motivate him to do his best for you.

When he knows that he's wanted, that his work is appreciated by the members of his group, when he knows that his efforts are contributing to the achievement of a common goal, then he becomes proud of himself, proud of his group, his superiors, his organization. He'll be motivated to fight for his team.

Develop this strong sense of teamwork in your men, and you'll be able to instill within them a feeling of organizational pride and loyalty.

When you can develop a strong feeling of pride and loyalty to your organization in every employee, your task as a manager will be made much lighter. When the chips are down, when your men are called upon to give forth with their best efforts for you, they'll respond and support you as members of a well-trained team.

Effective teamwork will motivate your men to a state of high morale and esprit, individual proficiency and organizational efficiency.

Effective teamwork promotes, and yet it also requires, a high state of morale and esprit. With a good team spirit, the individual members of the team will perform their tasks much more effectively.

The final organizational efficiency of each team gives every individual team member a feeling of accomplishment and security. Recognition of the team as a whole helps to satisfy the individual's need of recognition.

Train your men to work together as a team, and you'll motivate them toward a common goal, production for mutual profit!

Teamwork within a large organization is the key to successful accomplishment of the primary mission, to make a mutual profit. Teamwork must be developed, not only within departments and sections and divisions, but between and among them.

Teamwork starts at the top and bottom and goes in both directions at the same time. It must spread out laterally on the same level as well. All your employees must work together as one big team for the common good if you're to achieve the maximum results.

Give your men one common goal, and they'll have to work together as one team to reach it.

How It Works

Before you can ever train your men as a team, before you can even allow them to assume their places as members of the team, they'll have to be trained as individuals in their basic job duties.

Some of the biggest names in business and industry today conduct intensive training programs for their personnel, both sales and executive. For example, all Brooks Brothers salesmen have to take a special training course before they start work. In addition to possessing thorough knowledge of woolens—their manufacture, cutting, etc.—they must be complete masters of selling etiquette so they can approach their customers with dignity and courtesy. Sears and Roebuck has special manuals for its salesmen to study; new salesmen are quizzed over and over until their division managers are satisfied, and that's no easy trick, I can assure you.

Filene's of Boston, known as the world's largest specialty store, helped to establish a Lincoln Filene Professorship of Retailing in the Harvard Graduate School of Business Administration. Woolworth conducts intensive training programs for its junior executives. There are hundreds of others who've invested countless sums in training their employees.

I'm going to give you nine specific inexpensive methods you can use to train your own men so you can make this dynamic law of motivation work for you. If you'll use them properly to motivate your employees, you'll soon be able to reach every person in your organization in such a way that they'll want to do their best for you through their individual and their team efforts.

The Nine Keys for Application of the Sixth Dynamic Law of Motivation

1. *Supervise to see that your organization is carrying out the primary mission that has been laid down for you by your superiors.*
2. *Make sure that the required facilities and materials are made available to your men to accomplish that primary mission.*
3. *Insure that these facilities and materials are being properly used without any waste of time.*
4. *Make all activities of your organization meaningful and have all your personnel engaged in fruitful, profitable work.*
5. *Eliminate any duplication of efforts, jobs, and manpower that you find.*
6. *Each man must know the jobs of those with whom he normally works, to insure teamwork.*
7. *To stimulate proper cooperation and teamwork, every man*

must know the functions, requirements, capabilities, and the limitations of all other sections, departments, or divisions in your organization.

8. Promote teamwork by encouraging your men's initiative.
9. Your enthusiasm furnishes that spark of motivation so necessary for real teamwork!

Discussion of the Nine Keys for Application of the Sixth Dynamic Law of Motivation

1. Supervise to see that your organization is carrying out the primary mission that has ben laid down for you by your superiors.

Geographical decentralization can cause problems.

"Once in a while I tend to forget what my real job is," Warren Douglas, manager of the East St. Louis Gardner Machine Company Plant, told me. "You see, since I'm paid a salary for managing this plant, I sometimes lose sight of my real objective, to make a clear profit for the entire company. And that takes the teamwork of my employees here at this plant.

"But I get so tied up in office red tape and administrative operational methods and procedures, time and motion studies and industrial engineering problems, research and development, and all the rest that goes with managing a plant that manufactures industrial machinery, I often forget about the actual money that's involved.

"Usually I have to be brought back to reality by the teamwork of my own accounting department in the form of a quarterly profit and loss statement. A phone call from the president or the chairman of the board up in Ohio to remind me that I'm the leader of a profit-making team brings me back to life pretty fast, too.

"But honestly, it's all too easy to get yourself so wrapped up in the mechanics of running a plant that you forget why you're really doing it—*to make a profit!*"

2. Make sure that the required facilities and materials are made available to your men to accomplish that primary mission.

You must furnish the facilities and materials; your men must furnish the time.

"If your men are working overtime, if you're paying them premium pay, time and a half and double time, because you don't want to buy enough equipment and materials for them to use, you're throwing away dollars to save pennies," John Kelly, the production control manager for the Cornwall Glass Works in Houston, Texas, told me.

"It took our accounting section to bring that fact home to me," he said. "We needed to increase our production. I wanted to do it by working overtime. They wanted to do it by increasing the plant facilities and adding to the labor-force.

"It took a lot of their patience, cooperation, and teamwork from them to convince me, but they finally did it. Today I'm the first one in line to signal approval of a capital expenditure if it's going to cut down on overtime premium pay."

3. Insure that these facilities and materials are being properly used without any waste of time.

Want to motivate your boss? Save your men's time.

"One of the best ways a department head can build his reputation with me is to properly use the time of his own subordinates," the owner of a small furniture manufacturing company in Marietta, Ohio, told me.

"I've made the money, the materials, the facilities of my plant, and the manpower available to each department head so he can properly accomplish his part of the primary mission.

"The thing is, if he doesn't use the time of his men the way he should, if he's not getting results, he's throwing their time away. When he does that, wastes one single minute of his subordinates' time, he's spending my money foolishly and I take a dim view of that!"

4. Make all activities of your organization meaningful and have all your personnel engaged in fruitful, profitable work.

There's a difference between "necessary" and "nice-to-have."

"We don't mind paying out the right salary if the job's really required," Jack Smith, office manager for the Capital City Transport Company of Des Moines, Iowa, told me.

"The trouble is, so many of our department heads try to pad their personnel requirements with *nice-to-have* jobs. I don't like the idea of paying an office clerk a secretary's wages, or giving a shipping clerk a traffic manager's salary.

"And more important and to the point, neither does my boss! I'm still responsible to him for controlling the manpower costs of our administration. That's my contribution to the team effort."

5. Eliminate any duplication of effort, jobs, and manpower that you find.

The bigger the organization, the easier it is to happen.

The bigger the organization, the easier it is for duplication of jobs, manpower, and effort. Usually we think of such duplication happening in non-profit organizations or in government, but they can take place in large profit-making corporations just as well. I've seen plenty of examples of this in every kind.

If you do happen to find any positions in your organization that are not contributing directly to the accomplishment of your primary mission—*making a profit*—then get rid of those positions at once. Keep the man if you can, but by all means get rid of the surplus job.

It happens even in banks.

Of all places, you might not expect to find duplication of jobs or manpower in a bank. But it can happen there, too.

Sam Evers, senior vice-president of the Cattlemen's Bank in Colorado Springs, Colorado, told me of an incident that took place in his bank.

"We had a clerk on the first floor of our bank who filed small loan correspondence and reports," he told me. "One morning while going over some of her paper-work, I noticed an out-box on her desk which was labeled 'Out-going for Clark.'

" 'Who's Clark?' I asked. 'Don't we have a Miss Clark on the next floor up?' 'Oh yes,' came my answer. 'She gets all my carbons.'

"Curious about this, I went up to the second floor. It was like seeing a movie for the second time. The papers I saw in Miss Clark's files were the same as the reports I'd been going over downstairs, *but these were the carbon copies!*

"After we checked into it thoroughly, we found we were paying two people on two different floors for doing the same job. The only difference was that the girl downstairs was filing all the originals and the girl upstairs was filing all the carbons! Sounds ridiculous, doesn't it? But it actually happened.

"We kept the second girl, the carbon copy, but we got rid of her job fast. If we'd had better cooperation and teamwork between our departments, in this case, between floors, it would never have happened."

6. Each man must know the jobs of those with whom he normally works to insure teamwork.

Organize it, deputize it, supervise it.

Every department in your organization must be organized, deputized, and supervised in a clear-cut, clean, and concise way. This will help to avoid confusion, waste of materials, loss of time, and loss of profits.

Every position must be covered individually, laterally, and in depth, but without any unnecessary overlapping of duties and responsibilities or waste of manpower. When each man knows his superior's duties well enough to take over his position, you have strength in depth.

When all your personnel are cross-trained in every position at the same working level, you have lateral strength. By lateral strength, I simply mean this: If Smith and Jones and Brown are all working side by side, but all on different jobs, then Smith ought to be able to do the work of Jones and Brown, and Jones and Brown ought to be able to do Smith's work, and on around. Cross-training and lateral strength should handle any temporary shortages of manpower for you.

7. To stimulate proper cooperation and teamwork, every man must know the functions, requirements, capabilities, and the limitations of all other sections, departments, or divisions in your organization.

Use this technique so your men won't pass the buck.

Follow this principle and your men will develop a mutual trust and understanding. It will promote teamwork throughout your whole organization. Neglect it and your teamwork becomes too compartmented.

If your organization is too highly compartmented or divided, passing the buck becomes commonplace. Production can easily fall apart.

A complete understanding of the responsibilities and the duties of the other departments will keep your men from trying to shift the responsibility to another place.

Lack of teamwork causes loss of profit.

"We were going in the red in our Mid-Western Electric plant here in Kansas City month after month," Claude Vance told me, "and I was getting scared. Production superintendents don't keep their jobs very long that way. Big corporations, like Mid-Western Electric, don't hold still for losses in their branches. It's either produce and make a profit, or get out!

"Our scrap and waste in our building departments was terrible. We were hauling more out the back door to the city dump than we could sell out the front.

"I kept after my general foremen to cut down on this scrap

and waste, but I was getting nowhere. Everyone was too busy blaming the other fellow to clean up his own mess. I had them giving me daily scrap reports, weekly scrap reports, and monthly scrap reports. Complete waste of time.

"When I tried to check them out, I'd find that if Smith's report was low one week, then Jones's would be high. The next week, if Smith and Jones were both low, then Brown's or Black's would be up, and so it went, on and on.

"All they were doing was passing the buck back and forth between them with men physically trying to sneak scrap out of one department back into another. Of course, the total amount of scrap going out the back door never did decrease.

"At last I saw where I was wrong, too. Instead of trying to find out why we had scrap, I'd just been yelling at them to stop it. So instead of my departments operating together as one big team, I had seven general foremen all at each others' throats instead of cooperating and trying to help each other.

"Once we all got together, we were able to approach the problem with one common goal in mind, and we licked it. But it took a lot of cooperation, teamwork, and a mutual understanding of the other fellow's problems."

8. Promote teamwork by encouraging your men's initiative.

Initiative is one of the first steps in teamwork.

One of the best ways to encourage teamwork and to train your men as a team is to encourage their ingenuity and initiative.

Initiative is the action of taking that first step or making that first move. It implies responsibility for beginning the action as well as getting the job done.

To see what has to be done, to determine what should be done, and then to take the necessary steps to see that it is done, even in the absence of orders from your superior—this is initiative.

If you encourage initiative on the part of your men, they

will also take the necessary and proper action to get the job done for you.

Develop initiative by throwing down a challenge.

A good way to encourage creative initiative on the part of your subordinates is to set up a certain standard and then *challenge them to beat that standard.*

Many industries today use the incentive system of payment. By this I mean, a man is paid a base rate for producing an established standard, call it 100 percent. If he can figure out a way to beat that established standard, that is to say produce a 150 percent in the same length of time the average worker produces the base rate of 100 percent, then he's paid for his production, and not for his time.

For example, say a man were paid two dollars an hour for the established standard of 100 percent production, a previously set figure accepted as the normal rate of production for an average man. If John Jones can produce 150 percent every day on his job, he'll earn 24 dollars each day rather than 16. In other words, he'll earn three dollars an hour instead of only two per hour for 100 percent base rate production. The more he produces, the more he gets paid.

Will the incentive system work? Let's ask George Myers.

George is chief of the industrial engineering department for the Jones and Laughlin Rubber Corporation's plant in Denver, Colorado. As the chief, he is responsible to the plant manager for time and motion studies, establishing standard production rates, and the supervision of the incentive production records and reports.

"When we were on a straight hourly rate," George said, "we had all kinds of labor problems. Trouble all over the plant, even to the point of deliberate and malicious destruction of plant machinery.

"The men just weren't earning enough money. There was no real incentive for them to put out a good piece of work nor did it matter too much to them how much they produced in a day. They got paid the same at the end of the day, no matter what they did. They had no reason to develop any team spirit, to work together as a team.

"Then we decided to try the incentive system. In this method, a man is paid for everything he makes just as long as it's quality production.

"Now we still keep a base rate of 100 percent in there for him. You see, if something goes haywire, if the machinery breaks down, electricity goes out, or anything else happens that's beyond his control, then he still gets his base rate per hour even though he isn't producing anything.

"That way he's always guaranteed so much at the end of each day or each week. But with the incentive system, a good and capable man can many times double his pay.

"Now when it comes to teamwork, in the rubber business we have a very tricky operation called calendaring. It's a four to five man team affair. That team gets the crude rubber stock ready for the rest of the plant production.

"Our calendar crews had really been some sour apples, a lot of foul balls for us when we were on a straight salary basis. But this incentive system brought them right back on the first team again.

"Before they were stubborn and hard to get along with; now they're doing a bang-up job. They're using their initiative to beat the standard almost every day; the company's making money; they're making money; and everybody's happy about that."

Your men can beat the standard too.

These men George told us about used their initiative and their ingenuity and their teamwork to beat the established standard to take home a better pay check.

If you want your men to use initiative and imagination and ingenuity in their work, you'll have to offer them a chance to beat your standard, too. Offer them that opportunity and they'll work as a team to do just that. It's a challenge to them, and both of you will make more money.

Don't quibble over his incentive production.

If you're paying a man on an incentive basis for his production, don't quibble and try to get back his money after he's earned it by arguing with him about his quantity of production.

First of all, a man who's been on the job for several years ought to be able to earn a much higher percentage on his incentive production than a man who's just started to work for you. And if that old hand hasn't enough ingenuity and initiative to try and beat your established standard, you'll be better off without him anyway.

But don't try to pull the experienced worker's earnings down to that new employee's level or down to what you *think* it ought to be. Instead, pull that new employee's earnings up to the higher level. The more they produce for you in a given period of time, the more money all of you make.

If you think you're being cheated, then you haven't fixed your incentive system properly. If you have a way to check both the quality and the quantity of a man's production, then do so. And if you haven't, then you'd better put one into effect right away.

Be sure your system works.

Whatever method you use to check a man's production, just make sure it's accurate and equitable. Don't let your time study people or your industrial engineering department make enemies for you in your own plant. It can so easily happen.

I've seen too many production lines where management couldn't possible prove or disprove a man's incentive production reports. It usually happens where a man is producing something in bulk quantities which is immediately used up in other production. When a man is producing items or pieces, his production is usually easy to check. However, it can happen anywhere. There's always that five percent who'll cheat on you.

I've seen it happen in factories employing thousands of people, too. It doesn't happen only in small inexperienced companies. It also takes place in big corporations who are listed on the New York Stock Exchange.

You must use initiative too.

Your men will quickly unite behind you as a team when you run into new, unexpected, and difficult situations just as long as you yourself show initiative by your own prompt and decisive actions.

You can encourage this same attitude in your subordinate supervisors by giving them work to do which will require them to develop their own plans to finish the task properly.

Assignment of tasks to your subordinates doesn't end your job.

You haven't fulfilled your own responsibility just by assigning tasks to your subordinates. You can't sit back and relax, assuming that everything will be done, and that all is well.

Part of teamwork and training your men as a team is for you to supervise to see that the job is done. Your proper supervision will motivate your employees to do a good job.

Initiative helps to solve problems.

Now then. Closely associated with the idea of initiative is resourcefulness. This is the ability to solve a problem or to deal with a troublesome situation in the absence of what you might call normal or conventional means or methods.

Your organization must be designed, manned, and equipped to meet the normal daily situation and to solve the average daily problems. But ordinary methods can fail when a new or unexpected set of circumstances is met.

You must do something about it.

Inactivity or just passive acceptance of some unsatisfactory situation, just because you don't seem to have the usual means to solve the problem, can never be used as an excuse for a lack of initiative, resourcefulness, and ingenuity on your part. You simply cannot sit down and do nothing. The problem won't go away; it'll still be there when you get up again.

To help you and your men develop initiative and resourcefulness, I recommend that you practice these five guidelines daily.

1. *Always stay mentally and physically alert.*

You simply can't grasp the initiative or see what has to

be done if you're physically or mentally asleep at the switch or walking around with your eyes closed.

   2. *Train yourself to recognize what has to be done.*

Once you see what has to be done, then don't hesitate to do it. Don't wait to be told. Never use the excuse that you didn't know what to do because your superior had never told you.

   3. *Learn to anticipate.*

Think ahead. Plan ahead. By doing this, you'll reduce the risk of the unexpected to the bare minimum.

   4. *Look for responsibility.*

Many people try to look the other way when responsibility comes along. Don't be afraid. Look for responsibility and then readily accept it when the opportunity comes your way.

   5. *Be adaptable.*

Always be ready to adjust to new and changing situations. Develop your ingenuity. Don't be afraid to venture into the unknown. Always be ready to take that calculated risk. Look for answers and solutions to problems, no matter what the obstacle.

9. Your enthusiasm furnishes that spark of motivation so necessary for real teamwork!

Enthusiasm helps develop teamwork.

One of the finest ways to develop teamwork in your organization is to be enthusiastic about your own job. If you're really enthusiastic about your work, you'll have a sincere interest and a deep zeal about doing your job and doing it properly.

When you're motivated, that fact alone will tend to motivate others. Your enthusiasm will inspire others and motivate them to do their best for you.

What is enthusiasm?

Enthusiasm implies that you have a cheerful and an optimistic attitude. If you're enthusiastic in your work, you'll always try to do the best job you can under all conditions, no matter what those conditions might be. Your cheerful enthusiasm can set the example for others to follow.

Enthusiasm and optimism are especially important when you're doing detailed work that tends to become tedious, boring, and monotonous, or in any complex and intricate situation that requires you to have a great deal of patience.

What enthusiasm is not.

Some people have the wrong idea about what enthusiasm actually is. You don't have to go around bubbling all over the place, calling everyone *dear* or *darling* or *sweetheart*. Somehow I've never been completely convinced that this isn't just a shallow and forced attitude.

But a good smile, now, that's different. It can be worth a great deal sometimes. Doesn't cost you a thing either. It can be that spark of enthusiasm that's needed right then to motivate one of your men to do the right thing.

If you do want to develop a cheerful and enthusiastic attitude about your work and your organization, try following these seven guidelines. They might come a bit hard to you at first; after a while they'll be as much a habit with you as brushing your teeth.

1. *Know and understand every detail of your work so you can sincerely believe in what you're doing.*

Need more be said about this first one?

2. *Be optimistic.*

Keep a positive mental outlook on your work and on your life in general. Don't be a pessimist; don't be a chronic complainer about everything. Life is pretty much what you yourself make out of it.

3. *Explain to your employees why they have to do a certain job.*

Tell your men the why and the wherefore of every task you give them to do, especially the ones that seem dull, uninteresting, and distasteful.

If you'll do this, much of the unpleasantness can be taken out of an undesirable piece of work. Just make sure that the person knows why the job has to be done. If you can't explain that to him, you'd better check up on it. Does it really have to be done? Just how important is that job anyway?

4. *Always be quick to capitalize upon success.*

Enthusiasm can be contagious. Nothing will build enthusiasm in your men more quickly than success. Always let them know about the successful accomplishments of your organization.

5. *Keep enthusiastic even when things aren't going your way.*

It's so easy to be enthusiastic when you're successful and when everything is going exactly as you've planned it. But it's really tough to be enthusiastic when everything's piling up on top of you and you can't see your way out from under. That's when you really have to stay in there and keep right at it. Never, never give up.

6. *Don't let yourself become stale.*

If you want to keep up your enthusiasm about your job and your work, then never allow yourself to become stale. Set aside a short period each day when you can completely free your mind from all business matters.

Relax completely, even if it's only for a few minutes. But do it. Take off your mental shoes, and wiggle your intellectual toes freely for a bit. You'll snap back refreshed.

7. *Whatever you do, do it vigorously, cheerfully, and forcefully.*

Many an improper order has been brought to a successful conclusion by enthusiasm. I've often heard it said that it's scientifically impossible for a bumblebee to fly according to the laws of aerodynamics. Its body is too big and heavy for the size of the wing span, something or other like that anyway. But, if the bumblebee knew it couldn't fly, it wouldn't. But it doesn't, so it does.

So don't use half-way measures about anything. If that job's worth doing at all, it's worth doing or it shouldn't be done. If it's worth doing, then do it; if it isn't, then don't.

To Sum It All Up

Teamwork is the key to successful operation of any organization. It is one of the most effective tools a master motivator can use. Teamwork must start at the top and work its way down to the last person to be truly effective. Each man must know where he fits into the team if you want him to give his utmost for the group effort.

Effective teamwork requires a high state of morale, esprit, discipline, and individual proficiency. At the same time, good teamwork promotes all these, and in addition, it contributes to the total organizational efficiency.

Never neglect an individual's accomplishments in your emphasis of the efforts of the group as a whole. You must always weigh and balance these two. The recognition of the individual and the final accomplishment of the group are both important to you in your motivation of your employees.

When you give an individual the proper recognition that is his due, you'll help to satisfy his needs for attention and importance. By the same token, each person will also get a feeling of pride in his accomplishments as a member of the team. He'll gain a feeling of security about his job when your organization does well through its teamwork.

Recapitulation of the Nine Keys for Application of the Sixth Dynamic Law of Motivation

1. *Supervise to see that your organization is carrying out the primary mission that has been laid down for you by your superiors.*
2. *Make sure that the required facilities and materials are made available to your men to accomplish that primary mission.*
3. *Insure that these facilities and materials are being properly used without any waste of time.*
4. *Make all activities of your organization meaningful and have all your personnel engaged in fruitful, profitable work.*
5. *Eliminate any duplication of efforts, jobs, and manpower that you find.*
6. *Each man must know the jobs of those with whom he normally works to insure teamwork.*

7. *To stimulate proper cooperation and teamwork, every man must know the functions, requirements, capabilities, and the limitations of all other sections, departments, or divisions in your organization.*

8. *Promote teamwork by encouraging your men's initiative.*

9. *Your enthusiasm furnishes that spark of motivation so necessary for real teamwork!*

Dynamic Law #7

Make Sound and Timely
Decisions

Learn to make sound and timely decisions, and your men will be motivated to have confidence in your abilities.

You can motivate your employees to have confidence in your abilities when you make a rapid and accurate estimate of the situation and arrive at a sound and timely decision. You must gather all the facts, analyze them, make up your mind, and finally issue your order with complete confidence that you've made the right decision.

Your employees will be inspired to do their best for you when you demonstrate good judgment in your decisions.

If you're able to reason logically under the most trying of conditions and decide quickly what course of action is necessary to take advantage of opportunities as they come up, your employees will be inspired by your good judgment. They'll want to do a good job, too.

Your prompt and positive action will enhance your men's confidence in you as an able leader.

When circumstances come up that cause a sudden change in your plans, your prompt and positive action will build your men's confidence in you. If you're hesitant and indecisive, you'll cause hesitancy, loss of confidence, and confusion within your organization. Your actions must be prompt and positive to be fully effective.

Your men will be motivated to turn to you for advice and help.

Learn to make sound and timely decisions and your men will be motivated to turn to you for advice and help. You'll become known as the expert in solving problems. Such a reputation will build your stature throughout your organization.

How It Works

"What's the difference whether I'm right or wrong?" Harry Adkins, a general foreman for the United Rubber Company in Springfield, Missouri, asked me. "When I'm right, no one remembers. When I'm wrong, no one forgets!"

Well, true enough, it's always human nature for people to remember a man's mistakes and to accept his accomplishments as routine, matter-of-course, and all that, but still. . . .

Perhaps if Harry would practice the nine specific techniques I'm going to give you to make this dynamic law of motivation, making sound and timely decisions, work, he'd improve his batting average, too. Don't worry. In the long run, the right people will remember how well you do.

You see, if you'll apply these nine exact methods daily, you'll soon become known as the expert in your organization when it comes to making decisions and solving problems. Your employees will turn to you for advice and help. So help them, and you'll find that when you do, you'll motivate them to give forth with their best efforts in turn for you.

With that thought in mind let's move right along to these nine techniques which will make this dynamic law of motivation work for you.

The Nine Keys for Application of the Seventh Dynamic Law of Motivation

Make sound and timely decisions.

1. *To make sound and timely decisions to solve your problems, you must first always make an objective estimate of the situation.*
2. *So far as the time and occasion will permit, plan for every possible event that can reasonably be foreseen.*
3. *Enhance your judgment by being as technically and professionally qualified as possible.*
4. *Always give measured consideration to the advice and suggestions of your subordinates before making your decisions.*
5. *Announce your decisions in sufficient time to allow your subordinates to make their necessary plans.*
6. *Be decisive in all your actions. Decisiveness is primarily a matter of practice and experience.*
7. *Encourage your subordinate supervisors to make continuing estimates of the situation.*
8. *Make sure that your administrative staff, your junior executives, and other necessary subordinates know what your present plans and policies are.*
9. *Always take into consideration the effects of your decision on your subordinate supervisors and their men.*

Discussion of the Nine Keys for Application of the Seventh Dynamic Law of Motivation

1. To make sound and timely decisions to solve your problems, you must first always make an objective estimate of the situation.

You must be an expert in solving problems.

First of all, don't look at a problem as just another headache. Look at it as an opportunity for growth. Don't be like the old fellow who complained, "I pray to God for strength, but all He ever sends me are problems to solve." Is there any other way to grow and become strong? So regard your problems as opportunities disguised in work clothes.

In your position, you'll be expected to be an expert in solving a variety of problems of every imaginable kind. Problems that come up just can't be ignored by you; they won't disappear just because you turn your back on them and refuse to look at them. They'll still be there when you turn around again.

So you've got to deal with problems just as soon as you can by the most sensible means you can find and use. Attack them when they're small; don't give them a chance to grow.

No matter how hard you try, practicing the eleven dynamic laws of motivation won't keep all problems from coming your way. Of course, it'll help, but you're still going to have some problems to solve, and I don't care how efficient you and your organization are. And when you do have problems, well, you'll just have to know how to solve them, won't you?

You'll have to make sound and timely decisions about your own business and your own employees. Your ability as an executive, a manager, or a supervisor will be tested, and you'll not dare to vacillate and waver. You'll simply have to *make up your mind, reach a sound decision, and issue an order.*

Experience alone isn't enough.

In solving your daily problems, you'll soon find that you can't always rely upon your own experiences, your own observations, and your own infallible intuition.

Besides, one man's intuition is said to be nothing more than another man's transparency, so you can't rely on that alone. Your experiences, observations, and intuition just won't be accurate enough to guide you to a sound and logical decision each time. You'll need much more than these to make sound and timely decisions.

You see, making a sound and timely decision isn't just a matter of intuition, whim or fancy, impulse, inspiration, and that sort of thing. The only way you can make a sound and timely decision is to *first gather all the facts bearing on the problem.*

Next, *make a rapid and accurate estimate of the situation* based on all those available facts you've gathered. Then, *arrive at a sound and sensible decision.*

You can't hesitate.

"You've got to be able to reason logically under the most trying of conditions you can possibly imagine in my business," Jeff Barnes, owner of the Barnes Construction Company in Kansas City, Missouri, told me. "I can't spare the time to even sleep overnight on it. I've got to make my mind up fast.

"I've got to be capable of deciding quickly and accurately what actions will be required on my part to solve the problem and to take advantage of opportunities as they come my way. If you hadn't shown me this *problem-solving-process*, I don't think I could manage it. At least I never could before; I was always snowed under."

Well, if you're hesitant and can't make up your mind, as Jeff Barnes used to be, you'll be snowed under, too. What's more, you'll never be able to motivate your men effectively. You'll only cause them to be hesitant, too. They'll lose complete confidence in your abilities as an executive. You can't motivate them to do their best for you that way. They simply won't trust your ability to make a sound decision.

Problems are often more complex than they appear to be.

Most problems are often more complex than they appear to be on the surface at the first casual glance. Your past experiences can be very misleading if they cause you to look only at the surface of the problem. Do that, and you'll be tempted to make a snap decision or an educated guess, neither of which are of too much value to you. Actually, they're nothing more than *guesstimates*.

What causes most problems anyway?

Usually you'll find that most problems you run into are caused when you do not properly balance the scales of accomplishment of the mission and welfare of the men.

Always balance the scales of accomplishment of the mission and the welfare of your men! Do that, and 95 percent of your problems will disappear.

For example, if you use mass punishment because you can't find the guilty individual, you're not considering the welfare of all the men. Punishing all of them will only multiply your problem. Before you might have had only one problem; now you'll have as many problems as you have employees.

It's more important to find out *why* the problem came up in the first place, isn't it? You need to find *what* conditions caused your employee to do what he did. This is really your problem. Don't waste your time looking for the wrong thing.

The problem-solving process.

The problem-solving process has three main steps to learn and follow. These are:

1. *Recognize the problem.*

2. *Make an estimate of the situation.*

3. *Take the appropriate action.*

Now then. Let's take up these three steps in order. So first:
1. *Recognize the problem.*
You must clearly define and determine the limits of the problem that you've uncovered. What are its boundaries? What are its limitations? What is its exact nature? You must find all the pertinent details and gather up all the facts bearing on the case. Once you've determined *what your exact problem is,* you're ready to turn to the second step which is:
2. *Make an estimate of the situation.*
To make a proper estimate of the situation, you must follow these four sub-steps:

a. *Find out the exact cause of the problem.*

b. *Determine all the possible solutions.*

c. *Explore and evaluate all possible solutions.*

d. *Select the best solution.*

a. *Find out the exact cause of the problem.*

To determine the exact cause of your problem, you must find the answer to five specific questions:

1. *Who* is involved.

2. *What* are the exact circumstances, the precise conditions?

3. *When* did this problem first appear?

4. *Where* exactly did it happen?

5. *Why* or *How* did it happen?

You see, once you've isolated and defined your exact problem, you're ready to find out *who* is involved in this situation. You'll also want to know exactly *what* circumstances and conditions really do exist. You'll be concerned about finding out *when* and *where* it actually happened. And perhaps most important of all, you'll have to find out *why* or *how* this problem came up in the first place.

You'll also need to know what other facts bear on this problem or have a direct relationship to it. If certain parts of it can't be proven by factual evidence, then you'll have to make some logical assumptions. And this is one place where you'll be required to use properly your past experience, your good judgment and common sense.

b. *Determine all the possible solutions.*

The second sub-step in making an estimate of the situation requires you to determine all the possible solutions. Once you've figured out the underlying cause of your problem, you're ready to look at the various possible solutions available to solve it.

Don't rule out a possible solution on your first trial examination of it. Even if it doesn't prove worthwhile for solving today's problem, it might well be the answer for tomorrow's.

Always stockpile your ideas. They can be of value to you later on. The more possible solutions you consider, the better your chances that the one you select will be the right one.

c. *Explore and evaluate all possible solutions.*

The next step in making an estimate of the situation is to weigh the various courses of action by *comparing their advantages and their disadvantages.*

First of all, you must *weigh the advantages of a single solution against its own disadvantages*. After you've done that, you're ready to compare one solution with all the other possible solutions, weighing the advantages of one against the disadvantages of all the others.

Finally, you must decide which solution will be the most effective one for you to use in *solving this specific problem*.

    d. *Select the best solution.*

The last sub-step in part 2, making an estimate of the situation, is to select the best possible solution as I've indicated above.

Now then. This final solution that you pick can be one of the single solutions you've considered, or it can be a combination of two or more of the solutions you've had in mind. Don't arbitrarily limit yourself.

    3. *Take the appropriate action.*

The last step in the problem-solving-process is to take the appropriate action to solve the problem. Once you've decided which solution you're going to use, then *put it into effect immediately* by issuing the proper order.

Don't delay; don't tremble and waver with indecision and hesitation now. The hard work is over. Step right out with confidence and put your corrective action into effect at once. *Put your solution to work for you. Take the appropriate action. Issue the necessary order.*

    The problem-solving-process in summary then . . .

Making an estimate of the situation is certainly not limited to business, industry or the military services as some people suppose. It's a process that is used in the everyday life of every person. Such a simple matter as crossing the street takes an estimate of the situation.

Let me summarize these steps of the problem-solving-process for you briefly and rapidly now.

1. *Recognize the Problem.*

2. *Make an Estimate of the Situation.*

    a. *Find out the exact cause of the problem.*

    b. *Determine all possible solutions.*

    c. *Explore and evaluate all possible solutions.*

    d. *Select the best solution.*

    3. *Take the Appropriate Action.*

2. So far as the time and occasion will permit, plan for every possible event that could reasonably be foreseen.

Always be prepared for any emergency.

Always plan ahead for every possible event you can think of that might logically take place. Making sound and timely decisions depends primarily upon having a continuous estimate of the situation in your mind at all times. Luck, therefore, is what happens when preparation meets opportunity. Of course, *the problem is* that opportunity always looks bigger going away than coming.

3. Enhance your judgment by being as technically and professionally qualified as possible.

Judgment is a personal quality you'll have to develop.

Good judgment is a personal quality you'll need to develop if you want to make sound and timely decisions. It is that ability you'll need to possess so you can weigh logically all the facts and apply all possible solutions to the problem so you can make the proper decision.

To improve your judgment, you should be as technically and professionally qualified as possible. Education, experience, time, and common sense will all be important to you when the moment comes for you to use proper and good judgment in reaching your decisions.

Judgment must be completely unemotional. Just because you

don't happen to like the way a man combs his hair or the fact that Mr. Jones has a red-headed wife should never be allowed to influence your decisions one way or the other.

If you want to improve your ability to render proper judgment so you can make sound and timely decisions, then practice following these three guidelines:

(1) *Practice making estimates of the situation.*

Always look ahead. Anticipate those situations that require decisions from you if they would happen to come up. Then you'll be prepared to handle them if the occasion arises.

(2) *Don't make rash or hasty decisions.*

Spur of the moment or snap decisions made on so-called intuition, whim, or fancy are usually worthless. They're really nothing more than *guesstimates.*

(3) *Use common sense.*

To develop a sense of good judgment, approach your problems with an attitude of common sense and an understanding of people.

4. Always give measured consideration to the advice and the suggestions of your subordinates before making your decisions.

Ask for their recommendations.

"Not only do I give consideration to the advice and the suggestions of my employees," Randy Turner, general manager of the huge Shoppers Fair in Omaha, Nebraska, told me. "I ask for their recommendations. I always try to take advantage of their ideas and their experience.

"But once I've listened to their advice and my decision has been made and announced, then the time for any further discussion as to the merits of my decision has passed.

"From then on I require their full and whole-hearted support of my policies and my plans. The retail business here in Omaha is a tough business. I can't afford too many mistakes, or I'd soon be out of it."

5. Announce your decisions in sufficient time to allow your subordinates to make their necessary plans.

Let them know what you're going to do.

Don't surprise your subordinate supervisors by announcing your plans and your decisions to their subordinates. That's their job, not yours. Let them do it.

Don't leave your subordinate supervisors out on a limb by not giving them enough time to develop their own plans, reach their own decisions, and issue their own necessary orders to do the job for you.

6. Be decisive in all your actions. Decisiveness is primarily a matter of practice and experience.

Decisiveness is much more than just making an arbitrary choice.

Decisiveness is defined as that quality or that ability to make up your mind, to settle a dispute, to answer a question, to give a judgment of some sort. It implies firmness, determination, and direction of purpose and action.

Don't be emotional about it.

You should never allow your emotions to play any part in reaching your decisions. There's really no exception to this that I can think of at all.

For example, the promotion of a man should be based upon his abilities to produce for you, not upon some sentimental notion that he must be promoted just because he has a wife and eight children to feed, he needs money, and you really do feel sorry for him. We all need money, don't we?

True, emotion does play a part in some decisions we make. If we're talking about love and marriage, I'd agree immediately that emotion plays a part. But marriage is marriage. Love is love. And business is business! Of course, you need heart in your work, but not senseless emotion.

How Judge Edwards looks at emotion.

The Honorable Arthur Edwards, District Court Judge in Kansas City, Missouri, says that a jury is not entitled to use emotion. "A jury's duties require it to use judgment and decisiveness in reaching a decision as to whether the person is guilty or not guilty," says the Judge. "It's my prerogative to allow sentiment, heart, and emotion to enter the picture when I'm rendering an appropriate sentence if the man is found to be guilty. Mitigation is presented after the decision of the jury has been reached, not before."

Learning to be decisive.

Being decisive in your work and in your actions is largely a matter of practice, past experience, common sense and good judgment, and quite a little bit of courage.

To develop this quality of being decisive in your work so you can motivate others by your decisiveness, concentrate daily on these five guidelines:

(1) *Learn to be positive in all your actions and orders.*

Don't waste time and delay in making your decisions simply because you're afraid of making a mistake. Many times you'll be able to get rid of your fear and your needless worry about reaching the proper decision if you'll just cut away all the fringes, red tape, and trimmings that tend to clutter up the place and hide the main issue.

Reach right through the middle of all this debris; get straight to the heart of the problem. When you do, you'll usually find you can reach a quick and proper decision.

(2) *Get all the available facts bearing on the problem.*

Stick to the subject at hand. Don't clutter up your mind with facts and figures that have nothing to do with the problem you're trying to solve. Get the facts and then analyze them from every possible angle and viewpoint. Then, based on all the available data you've got, make up your mind. Reach a decision. Finally, issue your order with complete confidence in your judgment.

(3) *Recheck the decisions you've made.*

Recheck the decisions you've made and the orders you've issued only to see if they were sound, proper, and timely, and to see whether they're still fitting and correct to be kept in force. Don't recheck them just because you're afraid you might've made the wrong decision.

(4) *Analyze decisions that have been made by others.*

Analyze the decisions that have been made by other top people in your field. If you don't agree with what they said or did, find out why and where you disagree. See whether your reasons for disagreement are valid and logical. See if you've based your opinion on sound and solid facts.

(5) *Broaden your viewpoint.*

Broaden your viewpoint and improve your ability to be decisive by studying the actions of others so you can profit both from their successes and their failures.

A secret of making sound and timely decisions.

One of the secrets of being able to make sound and timely decisions and being decisive in all your actions stems from the ability to *concentrate fully on only one point at a time.* Sound hard to do? Listen to how Frank Bishop, owner of the Bishop Contracting Company in St. Louis, Missouri, does it.

"Actually now, no one on earth can do more than one thing at a time and do any of them very well at all," Frank told me. "But there is a way of doing it so that for all practical purposes other people will think you're capable of handling everything at once.

"And I don't know of any place where that ability is more needed than in the building and contracting business. There's always a hundred and one things to keep in mind. The clue to handling all those details is this:

"You must be able to focus your mind on only one specific subject as it is presented to you, *blotting out of your mind all previous thoughts about everything else!*

"Just take care of that one single problem when it comes up.

Then the moment you've solved it, the moment you've answered the question, *immediately erase it from your mind. Completely forget it!* That's the only way you can be mentally relaxed and ready to handle the next tough situation when it comes along."

Do only one thing at a time.

In other words, Frank is saying that you must keep your mind so flexible you can switch from one problem to another quickly without getting them all twisted and tangled up in your thinking. *Never drag the details of one problem into the details of the next problem.*

This is the only way you'll ever be able to handle many things at the same time, or at least, this is the appearance you'll give to others who watch you work.

The ability to do this is one of the true marks of the top-notch executive, the manager who's really going somewhere. It takes a lot of concentration and effort. Just remember this idea. Concentrate on a single point at a time. *Don't scatter your fire!*

7. Encourage your subordinate supervisors to make continuing estimates of the situation.

Your subordinate leaders must know how to make estimates of the situation from their own viewpoints. They must continue to make future plans for themselves, for their own departments, their own divisions or sections, and for their own subordinates.

8. Make sure that your administrative staff, your junior executives, and other necessary subordinates know what your present plans and policies are.

No communication—no action.

When you make your sound and timely decisions, be sure that everyone concerned is informed what that decision is. Don't let costly mistakes crop simply because you forgot to tell a key person your decision and your plan for action.

9. Always take into consideration the effects of your decision on your subordinate supervisors and their men.

Consider the long-range effects too.

It is not enough to consider just the immediate effects your decision will have. You must be able to predict what the long-range effects are going to be. Remember that a chain reaction of events will be set off when you announce your decision and your subordinate supervisors put your plan into action.

This is especially true in counseling your men.

You must definitely consider the long-range effects here. To make a sound and timely decision when you're counseling one of your men will test your ability and your skill to the utmost.

Just what is counseling anyway? Well, Dr. Ralph Reynolds, consulting psychologist for the Allied Chemical Corporation says that counseling is simply a matter of talking over a problem with someone else.

"The most effective form of counseling," says Dr. Reynolds, "is the kind where the person who has the problem figures out his own solution to it by talking his problem *out loud* to you.

"All you have to do to make it work is make yourself available. Lend a willing ear, show an active interest in the man's problem, and encourage him to talk freely.

"The end result of this kind of counseling is that the man either figures out a way to solve his problem, or he learns to accept it and live with it. Either way, you've done a good job of counseling by simply listening."

What kind of problems do your men have?

What kind of problems will your employees have? All kinds. They'll have complaints about position and jobs and promotion, discrimination of some sort, financial problems, family troubles, and on and on and on.

If you can't help a man solve his problem, you've got a dissatisfied worker on your hands. I don't care whether that problem he has comes from inside or outside your organization.

As long as he has a problem, his mind will never be free from worry. Certainly he can't concentrate on his job, and as a result, an outside personal problem has now become one that definitely requires help from someone within your organization.

To get rid of problems, start your own counseling program.

Make sure all your subordinate supervisors understand the need for a sound counseling program. Let them know the benefits to be gained for your organization by using a sound and active counseling system.

Have your subordinate supervisors make themselves available at every practical opportunity to give proper guidance and assistance to their men.

How to counsel a man with a problem.

First of all, you must have a sincere and understanding attitude. Keep in strict confidence any information that you gain during a counseling session with a man. Think of what he tells you as a privileged communication. Violate this principle, and you'll never have an effective counseling program. If your employees can't trust you, they'll never confide in you.

Get others to help you.

Always make full use of assistance that's available from your administrative staff, your personnel section, and other departments if they can be of any practical help to you. If you do send a man to another department with his problem, don't just refer him to that other department and then wash your hands of it. Give him the exact name of the person he's to see. Then follow up to make sure that his problem was actually taken care of. Show him that you're deeply interested. Continue to supervise.

Special care must be taken when you're counseling a person with a deep-seated emotional problem. In such special cases, counseling by someone who doesn't have the proper professional training can often do more harm than good. There are few laymen who are experts in handling deep-seated psychological problems. If you're not a psychiatrist or a psychologist, then don't pretend to be one.

"There's an exception to every rule," says Dr. Price.

Dr. Lewis Price, general medical director for Pacific Telephone says this about counseling persons with alcoholic problems:

"As far as laymen go, members of Alcoholics Anonymous seem to be somewhat of an exception to this general rule," says Dr. Price, "but only when they're dealing with other alcoholics.

"Just because they've recovered from their disease of alcoholism, that doesn't make them experts in anything except how to stop drinking. And even then, they can only tell someone else how they did it. Acceptance of the A.A. program depends entirely upon the individual with the drinking problem."

Alcoholism is a major counseling problem.

Many large organizations today do encourage a chapter or a group of Alcoholics Anonymous right within the corporation walls. Eastman Kodak, Allis-Chalmers, and duPont have pioneered this effort to help alcoholics and to support Alcoholics Anonymous.

The recovery rate for alcoholics through A.A. in large corporations is about 65 percent. This is quite a remarkable figure, especially when it's compared with a 2 percent recovery rate by other methods.

Alcoholism is important to you when you consider the welfare of your men and the efficiency of your organization. You'll find that alcohol causes more absenteeism than any other single reason, or actually, any combination of reasons. And absenteeism of your employees means loss of profit for you.

Don't make the other fellow's decisions.

When you counsel a man, don't make his decisions for him. Here your job is counseling, not deciding. But you must guide your discussion in such a way that the person being counseled will figure out his own workable solution. Any other procedure defeats the purpose of counseling.

To Sum It All Up

Learn to make sound and timely decisions and you'll motivate your men to trust you and have confidence in you. They'll be inspired to do their best for you when you show good judgment and common sense in your daily decisions.

The executive who cannot make a sound and timely decision will never be able to motivate his men to do his bidding. Further, his indecision will cause hesitancy, loss of confidence, and general confusion in his whole organization.

When circumstances come up that dictate a change in your plans, your prompt action will enhance your men's confidence in you. Constant study, training, and proper planning will help lay the foundation for professional and technical competence so necessary to make sound and timely decisions.

Recapitulation of the Nine Keys for Application of the Seventh Dynamic Law of Motivation

1. *To make sound and timely decisions to solve your problems, you must first always make an objective estimate of the situation.*
2. *So far as the time and occasion will permit, plan for every possible event that can reasonably be foreseen.*
3. *Enhance your judgment by being as technically and professionally qualified as possible.*
4. *Always give measured consideration to the advice and the suggestions of your subordinates before making your decisions.*
5. *Announce your decisions in sufficient time to allow your subordinates to make their necessary plans.*
6. *Be decisive in all your actions. Decisiveness is primarily a matter of practice and experience.*

7. *Encourage your subordinate supervisors to make continuing estimates of the situation.*
8. *Make sure that your administrative staff, your junior executives, and other necessary subordinates know what your present plans and policies are.*
9. *Always take into consideration the effects of your decision on your subordinate supervisors and their men.*

Develop a Sense of Responsibility in Your Subordinates

Develop a sense of responsibility in your subordinates, and you'll encourage a mutual confidence and respect between them and their superiors.

When you motivate your men by placing your trust in them to do the job, they'll respond with everything they've got for you. Increasing a man's responsibilities heightens his own confidence in himself and in his own abilities to do the job. He'll be proud of himself and of what he does for you.

You'll encourage each subordinate to exercise initiative and to give his wholehearted cooperation to the team effort.

When you offer a man the opportunity to use his imagination and ingenuity, he'll want to show you that your trust is well placed. Do this, and you'll help him to develop initiative and resourcefulness. His individual efforts will contribute markedly to the efforts of the team and the organization as a whole.

Show faith in your subordinates and you'll motivate them to accept greater responsibilities for you.

128

Whenever you show confidence in a man's work, when you show that you have faith in him and his abilities, he'll require far less supervision. He'll be motivated to work on his own, and he'll continue to work whether the boss is around or not. A man who will work only when you are around is worthless to you.

> *Develop a sense of responsibility in your subordinates, and you'll always have a pool of trained supervisory personnel available to you.*

Develop a sense of responsibility in your subordinates and you'll always have a man trained to take over his superior's job. You won't waste your time and money training and re-training men from the outside. You'll reduce your requirement of hiring supervisory personnel *off-the-street*.

How It Works

There are ten exact techniques which you can use to make this dynamic law of motivation work for you. Sears Roebuck, the J. C. Penney Company, Lincoln Electric, and many others have used these same techniques to build their own huge organizations.

For example, Sears Roebuck never hires its store managers *off-the-street*. They work their way up through the company. When one top man retires at Sears, no less than 14 others are promoted on up the line. How can they do this? By having developed a sense of responsibility in their employees.

The J. C. Penney Company has also developed this strong sense of responsibility in its managers and employees to the extent they are all called *associates*. It's a standard policy at Penney's that all must start at the bottom. Every top Penney executive has done so.

If you were to ask any Penney associate how the chairman of the board would be replaced if he died, the answer would be, "We'd hire a new office clerk!"

You can develop this strong sense of responsibility in your

subordinates, too, if you'll follow these ten key methods I'm going to give you. Use them, apply them daily, and you'll soon be able to reach every person in your organization in such a way that each of them will be inspired to give forth with his best efforts possible in line with his own individual capabilities.

The Ten Keys for Application of the Eighth Dynamic Law of Motivation

Develop a sense of responsibility in your subordinates.

1. *Always operate through your already established chain of supervision within your organization when you issue your orders and your directives.*
2. *Use mission-type orders to the greatest extent possible.*
3. *When you give a man the responsibility for doing a job, always give him the proper authority too.*
4. *Give your subordinate supervisors every opportunity you can to perform the duties of the next higher position in your management chain.*
5. *Correct their errors in judgement, initiative, and ingenuity in such a way that you'll encourage their continuing development of these basic personal qualities.*
6. *Be quick to recognize the successful accomplishments of your subordinates when they do demonstrate initiative and resourcefulness.*
7. *Give advice and assistance freely when you are asked to do so.*
8. *Always make sure your personnel are assigned to jobs where they have a chance to use their previously demonstrated or potential abilities.*
9. *Be prompt and fair in backing your men to the limit. Have faith in every subordinate.*
10. *Always be willing to accept the responsibility, and insist that your subordinate supervisors live by the same high standard.*

Discussion of the Ten Keys for Application of the Eighth Dynamic Law of Motivation

1. Always operate through your already established chain of supervision within your organization when you issue your orders and your directives.

Never by-pass your chain of command.

"Look at it this way," Ken Carter, safety director for the McLean Trucking Company of Sedalia, Missouri, said to me. "If you by-pass your chain of command or your channel of supervision when you issue your orders, you're saying to the man in so many words, 'I don't trust you to do the job!' You don't do that to good truck-masters and truck dispatchers and keep them."

You must always show your staff and your subordinate supervisors that you do have faith in them and that you expect them to do their best. People always tend to do what is actually expected from them. If they know you have the confidence in them to do a first-rate job and that you expect it, that's the kind of performance they'll normally turn in for you.

2. Use mission-type orders to the greatest extent possible.

Emphasize skill—not rules.

Why make a man stand to do a job if he can do it just as well sitting down? Yet I've seen supervisors and foremen and superintendents do just that. They were defeating their purpose, to motivate their men to do their best for them. No man will do his best for you if you insist upon following a rule just for the sake of following a rule. Have a reason for the rule in the first place.

Tell your subordinate supervisors what you want them to do. But don't tell them how to do it. Hold them responsible for getting the desired results, but not for the methods they use to get those results. Delegate and supervise, but don't intervene unless it's absolutely necessary.

Balance the scales.

Your limiting points are balancing the scales of accomplishment of the mission on the one hand and the welfare of your men on the other. Never place profits above the welfare and safety of your men, but by the same token, you can't place welfare and safety of your men ahead of successful accomplishment of the mission.

3. When you give a man the responsibility for doing a job, always give him the proper authority, too.

Authority and responsibility go hand-in-hand.

Whenever you give a man the responsibility for doing a certain job, you must also give him the authority to do it. *Authority and responsibility must go hand-in-hand.* You cannot separate them.

If you give the responsibility to your subordinate supervisor without giving him the proper authority to carry out that responsibility, you've violated a basic rule of management. You'll not motivate your men to do their best for you that way. Not only is it evidence of poor management, it's evidence of *no management.*

Give him an objective and a sense of direction.

Give your man a goal, aim him in the right direction, get out of the way. Once you've given him the responsibility and the authority to carry out that responsibility, then don't interfere with the operation unless absolutely necessary to do so. Here again, mission-type orders are the best to use to develop a strong sense of responsibility in your supervisors.

Use the J. C. Penney System

In the Penney system the store manager is the key man. He is held completely responsible for the operation of his store. By the same token, he's given full authority to run his store.

He hires and trains his own help. He decides what to do about his own local advertising. He orders most of his merchandise from lists and samples sent to him by the Penney headquarters, but he chooses what he wants. He's not required to accept items not suited to his own locality.

In short, he runs his own store on a completely decentralized system, with nothing more than gentle policy guidance from the top.

Don't get bogged down with details.

If you won't delegate work down to your subordinates, you'll soon be smothered in a mass of details. One of the major complaints of the average business executive today is being harassed by trivial detailed matters.

The average businessman or corporation executive today wastes from 40 to 70 percent of his working day by doing paperwork he should have given to someone else.

Why does he let this happen? He doesn't have the ability to organize his operation, or he's afraid to delegate the responsibility on down to his subordinates.

But in this highly technological and automated industrial world, you'll find you can't keep up with all the details. Today, you must have true organizing ability. If there's one thing industry and business look for today in a manager, it's the ability to *organize—deputize—supervise.*

Try E. Joseph Cossman's system.

Mr. E. Joseph Cossman, mail order millionaire, says this in his book published by Prentice-Hall, Inc., *How I Made $1,000,000 in Mail Order,* "Look at each piece of correspondence, think about it, make a decision, pass it along for action, file it, or destroy it . . . but never, never handle the same piece of paper twice. Your fidelity to this one rule will keep your desk clear."

4. Give your subordinate supervisors every opportunity you can to perform the duties of the next higher position in your management chain.

Work for strength in depth.

If you don't offer your qualified subordinate supervisors the opportunity to work in the next higher position, you'll never know what their real potential is. Take every opportunity to see what each one of them has to offer to you and your company for the future.

If economic expansion is to continue . . .

Giving a man the responsibility for doing a job and the authority to do it is one good way for a corporation to continue its successful growth. It must develop a strong sense of responsibility in all its employees if it is to continue its economic expansion.

Delegate authority with responsibility, and you'll develop a mutual confidence, trust, and respect between you and your subordinates. You'll be showing them you have faith in them and their abilities to do a better job for you. You'll increase their desires to take on more and greater responsibilities. In short, you'll motivate them to do their best for you when you give them added responsibility.

It's also just as important to find out which men cannot assume additional responsibility so you can get rid of them early in the game. Don't let them become your obligation by carrying them along, hoping they'll somehow learn to assume responsibility. A man either will or he won't and that's all there is to it. For example . . .

Meet Robert Horwith from General Motors.

Not long ago I had the chance to talk with one of the younger executives in General Motors' industrial relations department, Robert Horwith.

Bob and I were discussing how to use the dynamics of motivation in big corporations to get the best possible results from employees. He told me about one of their men who just couldn't make the grade when it came to added responsibility. In effect, here's just about what Bob told me.

"This Mr. Jones had been working for us quite some time in production," he said. "Been with us several years, in fact. Quiet and friendly, he seemed to get along well with everyone. Reliable, always on time, did a good job, that sort of thing.

"Scored high on intelligence tests, but he didn't seem to have that extra drive we're always looking for in management. Still, sometimes that spark doesn't show up until a man's in a job with some real challenge.

"That's about where Mr. Jones stood with us. A plugger—but we'd seen no spark yet. Anyway, a chance came for promotion for him. So we made him a production supervisor at a good healthy increase in his pay check. Naturally, he had more responsibility in his new job.

"Well, it didn't take too long to find out he just couldn't manage it. He couldn't take that added responsibility for the work of his men. And if a man's going to go up the ladder with us, he has to accept the responsibility for the mistakes of his men. Jones couldn't do that.

"We gave him every chance, for sometimes a man flounders around for a while before he grabs hold of a new job. But after two months he asked to be relieved. He wanted to go back to his old job on the assembly line.

"He'd developed a nervous stomach and was so worried about making a mistake, he couldn't sleep anymore. That production supervisor's job was too much for him. Couldn't take the added responsibility even though his pay was nearly double what it had been before.

"When he was referred to my department for help, I asked him why he wanted to go back to his old job. Here's what he told me: 'Mr. Horwith,' he said, 'I just can't give orders to other people. I'm afraid I'll make a mistake and tell them to do the wrong thing. Then they would laugh at me and make fun of me. I couldn't take that.

"'And another thing—I can't help the mistakes they make.

I've got enough troubles of my own without taking on any of theirs. Just put me back on my old job where I don't give orders to anyone. I just want to be at my old machine again.'

"Well, what could we do? We put him back on the assembly line, but he's no longer with us. Automation caught up with his job. Since he'd already shown us he couldn't accept more responsibility, we had no other choice. We let him go."

One of your primary responsibilities is this.

Selection and development of your subordinate supervisors will be of prime importance to you. Once you've picked out the men you want for specific jobs, then their development will become your constant concern and one of your greatest responsibilities.

Take advantage of every opportunity to teach them the principles of motivation and management. Teach them how to apply these dynamics of motivation in their daily contacts with their men. Only then will they become more useful to you in carrying out their duties and responsibilities.

5. Correct their errors in judgment, initiative, and ingenuity in such a way that you'll encourage their continuing development of these basic personal qualities.

Don't destroy a man's initiative.

Destructive criticism on your part will completely destroy their initiative. It will always cause your subordinate supervisors to adopt a *play-it-safe, security-first attitude.*

Whatever you do, never criticize or condemn a man in public. Reprimand your men whenever it's necessary, but do so only in private.

Always praise a man in public.

When it comes to praise though, this is really a completely different matter. Always be liberal in praising a man when he deserves it, and be sure that you do so openly in front of all his associates.

If you're ever in doubt as to whether praise or a reprimand should be given to a man, always praise him. If both are in order, praise him first, reprimand him second, praise him third. Never leave a man with a sour taste in his mouth.

6. Be quick to recognize the successful accomplishments of your subordinates when they do demonstrate initiative and resourcefulness.

People thrive on appreciation.

I could repeat this idea of showing a man your appreciation for a job well done a hundred or more times and still never say it enough.

I've never met a single person who didn't like to be complimented. And when you praise a man in front of his fellow employees, it has a multiple effect. Those listening will work even harder to get in that honored position of receiving praise, promotion, or financial reward.

Public praise will raise morale, increase an individual's prestige, and strengthen his self-confidence. All these are important factors in the development of self-reliant supervisors and employees for your company.

Always remember to use such phrases as: *I'm proud of you, What is your opinion? If you please, Thank you, I need you, I'm counting on you.* They'll work magic for you every time.

7. Give advice and assistance freely when you are asked to do so.

Help a man when he needs it.

"When my subordinate supervisors ask for my help, then I help them," said Ted Scott, who is the Director of Ground Safety for the Air Force Communication Service at Scott Air Force Base, Illinois. "But I don't reach in just to interfere in their work. I try not to over-supervise. When I help them, I don't try to take over their individual jobs when I do so. I try to let them save face, too. That's important to a man."

Get rid of the inefficient ones as soon as possible.

Don't carry the man, just help carry his load. If you carry the man, you'll have nothing but headaches from him. Help him carry his load in the beginning until he can manage for himself. Never carry him.

If you don't have faith in your subordinate supervisor's abilities, get rid of him. But before you take such drastic action, you'd better take an honest inventory of yourself.

Part of his failures might be your own fault if you haven't given him the proper authority to do his job. It might be that you've kept too tight a rein on the controls yourself. And large and successful corporations can't be developed when one man insists on keeping all the controls tied up for himself in his own hands.

Develop a sense of responsibility in your junior executives.

As I've mentioned before, most corporations today believe in bringing their top executives up through their own ranks. Rare are the cases of top management being hired into the organization from the outside.

If they're going to bring their top management officials up through the ranks then, they've got to develop a strong sense of responsibility in their junior executives, in their young supervisors.

If a man can develop this strong feeling of loyalty and responsibility to his organization, he'll definitely go up the ladder of management to higher positions. If he can't, he'll not last long, at least in the top management brackets.

You must know your men's individual characteristics.

You'll have to know each one of your subordinate supervisors extremely well. Some of them will require you to keep a tight check rein on them in your supervision of them. Others will be able to carry out their duties quite independently and capably. Some will be much more aggressive than others; others less so.

Use a push-pull system.

Some of your men will be overly aggressive, for they'll be spurred on by their desire or their obsession for personal prestige and gain. This is good so long as it's kept under a tight control by you. Uncontrolled, such over-aggressiveness can create many undesirable situations. The over-aggressive supervisor is usually inclined to be somewhat negligent and careless about the welfare of his men.

The under-aggressive supervisor often has to be stimulated to be more enterprising in his work and in his use of manpower. He'll normally be overly concerned about the welfare of his men. In fact, he'll often use that over-concern of his as an excuse for his failures.

Different personalities call for different techniques.

In recognizing the differences in your subordinate supervisors, you'll be able to use the proper and suitable techniques with each one of them to gain their confidence, their respect, their loyal cooperation and obedience, and their willing support.

But if certain of them can't be motivated to develop themselves, get rid of them. Replace them. No one is indispensable to you but you yourself. And don't be at all squeamish and backward about ridding yourself of inept subordinates or junior executives. Keep them around and you'll come in some Monday morning to find a new name on your own office door.

I'm reminded of that old saying that goes something like this: *One of us to go. Since I'm the boss, you'd better start packing.* Friendship and sympathy have no place in a decision such as this.

How problems can come up.

A problem can often come up when your subordinate supervisors have already been given the authority to make certain decisions, and then they fail to use that authority you've already given then.

In such a case, the subordinate supervisor lacks the necessary courage to make a decision. He'll pass the buck back up to you so you can solve his problem. This wastes time, especially when you've already given him the authority to make this on-the-spot decision himself.

Counsel him—guide him.

Counsel him; point out his error; remind him of his own responsibility. Give him a second and even a third chance. If he succeeds, you've gained a competent, qualified, and loyal subordinate. If he fails to rise to the challenge of added responsibility, get rid of him.

The welfare of any one individual cannot be weighed against the mission of your entire organization. To properly balance the scales of mission and welfare, you must remember that the welfare of *all the men* goes on the scales, not that of just one man.

8. Always make sure your personnel are assigned to jobs where they have a chance to use their previously demonstrated or potential abilities.

There are seven methods of development of young executives and subordinate supervisors.

As I've already indicated, it's just as important, if not more so, sometimes to find out those who are incapable, those who are not qualified to be in leadership and management positions, as it is to discover those who are qualified and capable of filling those positions.

Once you've gotten rid of the inefficient ones, here are the methods you can use to develop the survivors:

(1) Actively encourage a planned and well-rounded professional program for them. Help them to develop their potential abilities.

(2) Periodically rotate their duties so they can broaden and diversify their backgrounds. They must understand the

whole picture to go on up the ladder of management responsibility.

(3) Give them the opportunity to attend self-improvement courses and training courses if your organization conducts them. If not, pay part of their costs for further college or business school education in night courses.

(4) Personally give them instruction and wise counseling in personal motivation and management principles, procedures, and techniques.

(5) Delegate the maximum authority to them that is both proper and appropriate in consideration of their individual positions and responsibilities.

(6) Always operate strictly through your chain of leadership—command—management—motivation—when you issue your orders.

(7) Set high standards of performance and accomplishment by your own actions. You must set the example for them to follow at all times. You must always be correct and proper in your own conduct.

How to conduct this development phase for your subordinates.

During this development period you must keep a direct and personal relationship with your immediate subordinate supervisors. Let them know exactly what you want from them. Also, let them know if they are progressing satisfactorily in your eyes. They have a right to know if they're meeting your standards. Give credit when and where it's due. Always be careful to avoid any hint of favoritism.

If you do have a rapid turnover of personnel in key supervisory positions, you have a definite problem. Not only is their replacement an ever-present and pressing problem, but you've got some other kind of problem within your organization, too.

This rapid and constant turnover of qualified personnel has plagued the armed services now for years and years. Study some of their problems and you should find ways to solve your own. Remember that you create your own problems; most of theirs are created by Congress.

Always pay close personal attention to the four hallmarks of management—*morale, esprit, discipline, and individual proficiency*—of your key subordinate supervisors so you can define and isolate your problem.

Too rapid a turnover means you'll have to plan for and constantly train a stream of replacements for each supervisor's position so you'll always have depth in your organization. And that's an extremely costly process.

9. Be prompt and fair in backing your men to the limit. Have faith in every subordinate.

Unless proven otherwise . . .

Unless it's been proven otherwise by their actions, have complete faith in your men. If you don't support your subordinate supervisors, and try to shift the responsibility which is rightfully yours to their shoulders, you yourself are shirking the duties of your management position.

10. Always be willing to accept the responsibility, and insist that your subordinate supervisors live by the same high standard.

Be one of the 5 percent.

Only 5 percent of every 100 people are willing to accept responsibility. Only 5 out of every 100 become successful in their motivation of others. 5 out of every 100 become successful executives, successful managers and leaders. 95 out of every 100 do not. 95 out of every 100 are only followers. So. Become one of those top 5 by accepting and fulfilling your responsibilities.

Your success or failure in this highly competitive business world will depend to a large extent upon just how effective you are in getting the best results out of your subordinate supervisors, your junior executives. Do you know how to motivate them to do their best for you? Have you been able to develop a deep sense of responsibility in them for you and your company?

Here's one way of doing it.

If you can get every one of your employees, and especially your young junior executives in minor management positions, each one of your subordinate supervisors, to think in terms of *this is my company,* then each of them will approach every situation and every decision as if he were the sole owner of your company.

How Lawrence Hall does it.

"One of the best ways I've found to develop a sense of responsibility in my men is to get them to buy a few shares of stock in the company," Lawrence told me. Lawrence is president of the Hall Aluminum Gate Company in Joplin, Missouri.

"That way, every time I tell a man what I want him to do, he looks at me with a brand new look. You know what he's thinking about now? He's thinking about how my order affects him, not so much as an employee, but as a stockholder! It's one of the best ways I know to get a man on your side."

You can't develop responsibility in a computer.

Some people think the day is coming when computers will run everything for us. But it's still going to take brains and ability to figure out just what kind of data has to be fed into those computers. And you can't motivate a computer either; you still have to motivate the man who feeds the computer.

Jimmy Black, an electrical engineer from Belleville, Illinois, installs these modern marvels of machinery for IBM. He told me that people many times expect far too much from their computers.

"A lot of people think computers are infallible," he said. "They can't understand what goes wrong when they don't get back the answers they want or they expect to get from the machine.

"Well, what went wrong? Simply this," he went on. "They fed the computer *GIBO—GIBO* instead of facts. Plain old *GIBO.*"

"What in the world is *GIBO?*" I asked Jimmy.

"GIBO? Oh, that's an abbreviation we use all the time in the computer business. It means *Garbage In—Garbage Out!"*

To Sum It All Up

If you delegate authority which is commensurate with the responsibility you give a man, you'll develop a mutual confidence and respect between you and your subordinates. They'll be motivated to do their best for you to get the job done.

Such delegation of authority and responsibility will encourage your employees to exercise their initiative and ingenuity, and to give you their whole-hearted cooperation.

Whenever you delegate authority, you've shown that you trust a man. You have faith in his judgment; you've given him a vote of confidence. He'll respond by asking you for more responsibility which is what you're after in the first place.

Recapitulation of the Ten Keys for Application of the Eighth Dynamic Law of Motivation

1. *Always operate through your already established chain of supervision within your organization when you issue your orders and your directives.*
2. *Use mission-type orders to the greatest extent possible.*
3. *When you give a man the responsibility for doing a job, always give him the proper authority, too.*
4. *Give your subordinate supervisors every opportunity you can to perform the duties of the next higher position in your management chain.*
5. *Correct their errors in judgement, initiative, and ingenuity in such a way that you'll encourage their continuing development of these basic personal qualities.*
6. *Be quick to recognize the successful accomplishments of your subordinates when they do demonstrate initiative and resourcefulness.*
7. *Give advice and assistance freely when you are asked to do so.*

8. *Always make sure your personnel are assigned to jobs where they have a chance to use their previously demonstrated or potential abilities.*
9. *Be prompt and fair in backing your men to the limit. Have faith in every subordinate.*
10. *Always be willing to accept the responsibility, and insist that your subordinate supervisors live by the same high standard.*

Seek Responsibility and Take Responsibility for Your Actions

When you seek responsibility, you'll learn to take the initiative in the absence of orders.

Always take the initiative. Don't wait for your company or your boss to tell you what you ought to do to qualify for advancement. The responsibility for development of yourself and your individual talents is your own.

When your men know that you are willing to step forward, actively seeking responsibility, even in the absence of orders, they'll be motivated to have confidence and trust in you and in your decisions and orders. And so will your superiors.

By seeking responsibility, you'll develop yourself professionally and you'll increase your leadership ability.

Actively seek every bit of responsibility that you can possibly handle. Accept it eagerly. You'll never go up the executive ladder by avoiding the tough assignments.

When you do seek added responsibility, you'll raise your own confidence in yourself and in your own abilities to do the job.

Your superiors will have added confidence in you, too, and so will your men.

Seeking responsibility will gain for you the respect and the confidence of your employees.

Men always respect a superior who has the courage to take a few chances, make a sound decision, and accept responsibility. Men who don't take chances, men who don't stick their necks out once in a while, will never become leaders and motivators of others. Men always despise a superior who does nothing more than *pass the buck*. Even if you're wrong, even when you make a mistake, they'll still have respect for you and they'll still have confidence in you simply because you had the courage to try.

When you seek responsibility and take responsibility for your actions, you'll gain the willing obedience, the loyal cooperation and the full support of all your employees.

When your men know that you're not trying to evade responsibility, when they know you're willing to take the full responsibility for their actions, you'll be able to gain their willing obedience, their loyal cooperation, and their full support. You'll be able to motivate them, then, to do exactly what you want them to do.

Whenever you seek responsibility, responsibility will seek out you.

Look for responsibility and responsibility will always find you. Leaders seek out responsibility and responsibility always finds leaders. No one can become a successful executive, a top-notch manager or leader unless he seeks out the opportunity for added responsibility. Waiting for responsibility to come your way is not enough; you must get out and look for it!

How It Works

There are 13 exact techniques which you can use to make this dynamic law of motivation work for you. Use them and apply them daily and by your actions you'll motivate your employees to do their best for you.

Most people look for privileges first, responsibilities last. If you want to succeed, it can never work that way at all. Look only for responsibility; privilege will follow automatically.

The Army, and the other services, too, I imagine, has often used the expression, *RHIP*, which means "Rank hath its privileges." However, it could just as readily be translated *"Responsibility* hath its privileges," which would be just as accurate, perhaps, if not more so.

This whole idea of accepting responsibility was summed up aptly by President John F. Kennedy in his inaugural address on January 20th, 1961, when he said, ". . . ask not what your country can do for you; ask what you can do for your country."

Always seek responsibility in your work. You'll find it's one of the best ways to motivate your men to seek responsibility for themselves in their work, too. By this simple act of seeking responsibility, by not passing the buck, you'll motivate your men to give out with their best efforts for you. And you'll develop professionally, too. So work hard. The job you save may be your own!

You've probably heard it said there are three kinds of people in this world: Those who make things happen; those who watch things happening; those who don't know that anything's even happening!

Be one of those who make things happen by seeking out responsibility and by taking responsibility for your actions.

The Thirteen Keys for Application of the Ninth Dynamic Law of Motivation

1. *You must learn your profession from the ground up while you are developing your capacity for accepting heavy responsibilities in the future.*
2. *Learn the duties of your immediate superior thoroughly, and be prepared to accept his responsibilities on a moment's notice.*
3. *You must be physically, mentally, and psychologically qualified to shoulder heavy responsibilities.*

4. *Always seek diversified management assignments so you can gain and develop a broad experience in the acceptance of responsibility.*
5. *Take full advantage of every opportunity that offers you an increased responsibility.*
6. *Perform every task, large or small, to the best of your ability.*
7. *Accept just and honest criticism and admit your mistakes.*
8. *Stick to what you think is right; have the courage of your convictions.*
9. *You must assume full responsibility for the failures of those who work for you.*
10. *Carefully study, analyze, and evaluate a subordinate's failure before taking any corrective action.*
11. *You must assume complete responsibility for your own actions.*
12. *Assuming the responsibility for what you fail to do is just as important as assuming the responsibility for what you do.*
13. *In the absence of any standing orders, seize the initiative and take the action you believe that your superior would direct you to take if he were present.*

Discussion of the Thirteen Keys for Application of the Ninth Dynamic Law of Motivation

1. You must learn your profession from the ground up while you are developing your capacity for accepting heavy responsibilities in the future.

This requires a lot of patience.

It's hard to be patient when you think you're smarter than your own boss, now isn't it? But this attitude reminds me of the saying, "I'm not young enough to know everything."

So you must be patient enough to take the long-range view of your future without feeling that your great talents for responsibility and authority and leadership are being wasted and frittered away. If you're that good, rest assured someone is going to notice you, and a lot sooner than you think, too.

Consider the young army lieutenant.

I think most of you know—but some of you may not, and I wouldn't want any of you to miss the point—so let me say that when an officer is first commissioned in the Army, he always starts off with the rank of a second lieutenant.

Then he enters upon an 18 month period of apprenticeship so he can learn what he's really supposed to do as an officer in the Army. If he's really lucky during this year and a half period of painful apprenticeship, he'll be mothered along by some patient old first sergeant who will tactfully and diplomatically (sometimes—sometimes not) guide his steps along the right road.

And at the end of that year and a half, he'll be eligible for promotion to the exalted rank of first lieutenant, that is, if he's learned his lessons well enough.

Meet Colonel Harrison Ryan.

A crusty old army colonel I used to know, Colonel Harrison Ryan, used to consider a second lieutenant's rank about the closest equivalent to nothing he'd ever seen. I doubt seriously if he ever once remembered that once upon a time, he, too, had been a second lieutenant himself.

If he did remember, he evidently didn't want to, for when he finished pinning a first lieutenant's silver bars on the shoulders of a newly promoted second lieutenant in his office, he would shake hands with that brand-new first lieutenant (which took a lot out of him, I think) and he would shout, "Welcome to the Army's Officer Corps!"

Increase your knowledge.

It takes a lot of work to accept responsibility and to become successful. In fact, I've heard it said that successful people are those who've made a habit out of doing the things unsuccessful people don't like to do. You know, there are always too many people who reach for the stool when there's a piano to be moved.

Now the continual acquisition of knowledge, not only about your own particular profession, but about the wide scope of business and industry in general is one of the wisest methods to use to prepare yourself for future responsibility. It also takes a lot of effort.

In fact, the accumulation of solid factual knowledge is a basic and essential tool of the successful person, whatever his field. But even beyond knowledge there lies wisdom, and to gain the insights that go with wisdom requires much study and much more reading. To increase your specialized knowledge and to gain deep wisdom from a broad point of view for the long haul, follow these eight guidelines:

(1) *Keep a personal library in addition to your business files and your business library.*

Don't be just a book collector, though. Buy those books that you know will be useful to you. So many people buy books for their libraries just to impress their friends and their neighbors. Don't buy your books that way. Buy those which you know you'll read and use for reference.

(2) *Study all the available literature and publications about your own business, your own vocation, your own profession.*

Make sure that you keep yourself up to date on all the current developments in your own field. Don't date yourself by stopping your education on graduation day. Libraries do admit adults as well as children, you know.

(3) *Keep yourself well read on other subjects as well as those of your own profession.*

This will help you to keep your mind alert and aggressive, sharp and active. If you confine yourself only to the trade magazines of your own professional interests, you could become so narrow-minded and so short-sighted that you'll be able to talk and think of nothing else. Don't be a bore to others.

(4) *Keep up with what's going on in the world.*

Keep yourself posted on current news events and political and government trends. Be an informed person. With today's communication facilities, it's completely inexcusable not to be well informed.

(5) *Form the habit of developing serious conversations so you can develop your mind.*

I'm not implying here that you ought to become an armchair psychiatrist or a fireside war strategist. I'm simply saying this: there's a lot more to talk about than just the weather, the time of day, or how you and the other fellow feel.

(6) *Analyze your own experiences in the light of the experiences of others.*

Compare and analyze; analyze and compare. Don't be so egotistical that you think you're the only person in the world who's had some tremendous experience. A close friend of mine has the disconcerting habit of upsetting the smug composure of stuffy ministers. When they get a little too self-righteous, he says to them, "You say you're an emissary from Heaven? May I see your credentials, please."

(7) *Always be alert and ready to learn.*

Listen, watch, learn from the mistakes of others. If you don't understand certain ideas, don't give up and quit just because you can't grasp them at first. Broaden your viewpoint and your own understanding by forcing your mind to work.

(8) *Develop your capacity to grasp new concepts and new ideas readily and rapidly.*

Try to look into the future beyond your own present point of view. Don't reject the ideas of others just because you didn't happen to think of them first.

It might well be that little in this old world is new, but a brand-new application of the old principles and old ideas can often lead to an entirely different and fresh approach with extremely profitable results.

2. Learn the duties of your immediate superior thoroughly, and be prepared to accept his responsibilities on a moment's notice.

Be ready for the tap on the shoulder.

If you're the boss's deputy, and you aren't prepared to take over his job in his absence, you'll not be his deputy for long.

Any variety of reasons can cause your chief to be absent. Sickness, hospitalization, vacations, personal business, promotion—any of these can force you to face up to being promoted, temporarily or permanently, or be passed up. It's all up to you.

Mr. McGrath says this about civil service promotions.

Mr. Wilbur McGrath, Civilian Personnel Officer, and the Director of all Civil Service activities at Whiteman Air Force Base near Warrensburg, Missouri, says this about promotion in the government.

"A lot of our section chiefs today here at Whiteman still don't understand the principles of civil service promotion." For example, just recently, one of the section heads felt his assistant was classified one grade lower than he should be.

"Now he told me all sorts of good things about his assistant. He told me that his assistant had been in that job for 5 years. Good; that meant he had plenty of experience. He said that he was responsible for the work of 21 other employees. Fine; that told me that he had supervisory abilities. He mentioned that the highest grade under his supervision was a GS-7. Excellent; I had nearly all I needed for his promotion, but not quite.

"You see, he forgot the most important point of all when it comes to promotions of assistants and deputies. And that point was simply this. *What additional duties does that assistant perform in the absence of his chief!* That's the key to the whole affair. And without that information, I had to turn down his promotion. I could do nothing about it."

3. You must be physically, mentally, and psychologically qualified to shoulder heavy responsibilities.

You must consider your health—your company will!

Are you highly energetic at all times? Do you have such good health and vitality that you can work long hours without tearing down your body and ruining your physical efficiency? Are you mentally and psychologically prepared to work more than the so-called minimum of 40 hours a week?

Your health will be a big factor to consider in your future promotions. Just think back to our presidential elections, for example. The health of the presidential candidates can greatly influence the voters of this nation.

And once elected, the President's health becomes even more important. The public gets a daily blow-by-blow account of how the President is feeling. When he has even such a simple ailment as a cold or a sore throat, everybody worries: the stock market sags; sales decline; everyone proceeds with extra caution.

Guard against the success diseases.

Did you know that certain diseases are tagged or labeled as the *success diseases?* The three leading success diseases today are high blood pressure and heart trouble, peptic ulcers, and nervous disorders. Alcoholism is running a hot fourth at the moment.

I think you can learn how to avoid all these though. It's really a simple matter of learning how to *pace yourself.* You've got to know when to start and when to stop. Learn the danger signals and the red warning flags and then watch for them along the way. Learn when to call a temporary halt, for sometimes continuing the race can be wholly disastrous to your health.

4. Always seek diversified management assignments so you can gain and develop a broad experience in the acceptance of responsibility.

Successful managers know no boundaries.

Top-flight managers know how important it is to broaden their overall training so that they are completely familiar with subjects outside their own initial areas of specialization.

The real top-notch executive can switch readily from one kind of business or industry to another without any loss of effectiveness. One of the best examples of this adaptability and flexibility is Mr. Don G. Mitchell, who at this particular moment is the Chairman of the Board of General Time Corporation.

However, I wouldn't guarantee this position a week from now for Mr. Mitchell has been highly successful in the publishing trade, the manufacture of containers, merchandizing, a soft drink company, an electronics company, and a utilities company of which he became president.

Mr. Mitchell has moved from his initial specialized activity into an area of such broad service that his talents are always in demand.

5. Take full advantage of every opportunity that offers you an increased responsibility.

You can't push a piece of string.

To get somewhere you've got to honestly and conscientiously seek out and welcome more and greater responsibilities in your work. Do you actually do this?

For example, when your boss looks around for someone to handle a really difficult piece of work, when he needs someone who isn't afraid to tackle a rough tough job, does he pick on you? Do you step forward offering to help him out? Or do you try to hide in the background, hoping he won't notice you?

Remember this now. A leader can't lead from behind; he has to be in front if he's going to lead. Trying to lead your men from behind their backs is like trying to push a piece of string. It just can't be done.

Follow President Truman's example.

When President Roosevelt died on April 12, 1945, Mr. Truman was sworn in as the chief executive, asking newspaper friends to "pray for me." He knew his limitations, especially since President Roosevelt had not brought him up to date on any major domestic or foreign problems since the election five months before.

It is doubtful that any President ever entered the White House more unprepared than President Truman, through no fault of his own. But he rose to accept his responsibilities in short order.

A small sign that he used to keep on his desk during his Presidency is the finest example of his full acceptance of his added responsibility. That little sign said, *The buck ends here.* It can't be said any simpler, yet any plainer than that, now can it? *The buck ends here.*

6. Perform every task, large or small, to the best of your ability.

Little things are important too.

Nothing can be done except little by little. And if you can't be trusted to do the little things, your boss will never entrust you with greater responsibilities.

I don't care whether the job you have is large or small, interesting or dull, important or seemingly useless to you. By doing the best job you know how, by covering every possible tiny detail of that job, you'll be rewarded by increased chances for promotion and advancement. But know this, too: It will be absolutely impossible for you to be promoted to a higher position if you don't show what you can do in your present job.

Be reliable in the smallest of tasks if you want bigger ones.

Reliability is a personal quality you'll need to develop if you want to motivate both your superiors and your subordinates. Reliability means to be trustworthy and dependable. It means that you'll always do what is required to be done with only the minimum supervision from your immediate superior.

Reliability can also be defined as your superior's faith in your present and your future performance of duty based upon the known facts of your performance in the past.

If you want to be thought to be reliable, your boss must be able to depend upon you to carry out actively, willingly, intelligently, and immediately his orders and his directives in all things, both big and small.

Now you'll notice that I've used four big words here telling you how to carry out your superior's orders and directives. I meant to use them. These words again are: *actively, willingly, intelligently, immediately.*

Just keep those four in mind when you're carrying out your orders, especially those which you don't think are quite right, and I'll guarantee you'll always be thought to be reliable in your work. Your boss will always be able to depend on you.

Now to be reliable, to willingly and voluntarily carry out the will of your superior, does not mean that you're supposed to give him your blind obedience. Blind obedience from you can easily lead to trouble for him. He should listen to your suggestions and your advice just as you must listen to the ideas and opinions of your own subordinates.

Once he's listened to your suggestions and given due consideration to your ideas, you're entitled to nothing more from him. When he makes his final decision, even though it might be the complete opposite of your recommendations to him, he is then entitled to your complete, whole-hearted, and energetic support. Don't you expect the same thing from your own subordinates?

Command can never be by conference.

The time for discussion is before a decision has been reached. Once the decision has been made, the time for discussion has ended. Now the decks must be cleared for action. *Command can never be by conference. Only one man can make the final decision.* If you are that man, make the decision. If your boss is that man, then support his decision.

If you want to develop reliability, follow these five guidelines:

(1) *Never make excuses; never alibi; never blame others.*

(2) *Do every job to the best of your ability.*

(3) *Be exacting and precise, especially in the minute details of your work.*

The tiny, monotonous, and tedious things are important to do, or they shouldn't be there in the first place. If they're important, do them, regardless of size. If they're not important, get rid of them.

(4) *Be punctual.*

Form early in life the habit of always being on time. Being late indicates carelessness and a lack of self-discipline and self-control. You can't be late and be thought to be reliable.

(5) *Carry out the intent and the spirit as well as the letter of the order.*

If you do what you're told to do grudgingly and with resentment, you're going to let yourself down sooner or later. If you feel there's some sort of conflict between the letter and the spirit of the order given, get a clear ruling on it from your superior. Once you've gotten your interpretation from him, stop quibbling. Accept his decision with good grace.

7. Accept just and honest criticism and admit your mistakes.

You'll need a thick skin.

"If you're thin-skinned, you'll never make it to the top," Fred Barlow, a member of the board for Dayton Rubber Company, told me. "As a manager, as an executive, nearly everything you do, everything you say, and almost everything you think will be exposed to public view.

"You'll be closely watched and criticized by your superiors, your subordinates, your associates, and worst of all, even by those whom you were so sure were your real friends. You can't afford to be thin-skinned in this game. If you are, you'll never make it."

Don't try to bluff your way through.

Honestly admit your mistakes without becoming irritated about it. Don't try to bluff and cover up; don't pass the buck. Do that, and you're only evading your responsibility. When you're president of the corporation or the chairman of the board, where do you pass the buck then?

8. Stick to what you think is right; have the courage of your convictions.

Don't be just a Yes-Man.

Stick to what you believe is right. Don't be just a yes-man in your work and in your organization. You won't last long if you say *yes* to everything. Have the courage to say *no* when it's necessary.

Tell your superior what he has to hear, not what you think he wants to hear. That can be a hard principle to follow at all times, but it has to be done if you want to live with yourself. It's hard to face yourself each morning in the mirror otherwise.

9. You must assume complete responsibility for the failures of those who work for you.

Can you take a rap on the knuckles for someone else's mistakes?

Taking the blows for someone else takes a lot of doing. It takes both courage and character. It's hard enough to be criticized by your superior for your own mistakes; but when you have to take the blame for what others have done, or haven't done, well, can you honestly manage to do that? It must be done, you know, if you're going to be the manager, the executive, the motivator and the leader.

It's like being an insurance company.

You could liken this to insuring your car. Your insurance company agrees to take the responsibility for your actions and guarantees to pay for your mistakes, no matter what they are and no matter what you've done.

If they don't support you when the time comes when you really need the help, they're of no value to you whatever. They just haven't earned their pay when they took your insurance premium.

And that's the same relationship that has to exist between

you and your men. When you're their leader or their supervisor, you've got to take the responsibility for their actions. And if you don't carry that heavy responsibility when the time comes, then you haven't earned your right to your bigger pay check, either.

You're no better than the insurance company who doesn't pay off when you have an accident if you won't accept the responsibility for the mistakes of your men.

10. Carefully study, analyze, and evaluate a subordinate's failure before taking any corrective action.

Whose fault is it?

First of all, make sure that his mistakes aren't due to your own failures in your position of management. Consider all the facts bearing on the case. Salvage the person when possible; replace him when necessary.

When you do have to get rid of inefficient and lazy personnel, then do it impersonally. Don't use your heart here. Use your heart where it will pay dividends for all of your men. The welfare of your entire organization is more important than the welfare of any one individual.

11. You must assume complete responsibility for your own actions.

Don't blame someone else for what you've done.

Can you keep from shifting the blame to others when you've made the mistake? Will you be willing to take the responsibility and the initiative to correct a bad situation? Or will you just sit down on the job and immediately blame your superiors, or worse yet, your subordinates? Remember this: Just take your own responsibility on your own shoulders, and you'll have no room left for chips.

The difference between a leader and a follower is the acceptance of responsibility.

Accepting responsibility for one's own actions is one of the biggest differences between a leader and a follower. Some people can't seem to grow up and take on responsibility for what they do, and it doesn't really matter how old they are in calendar years either.

Maturity is usually a matter of mental growth, not just physical growth. People who either can't or won't accept responsibility for their own actions just can't think for themselves, or they won't.

They don't want to do anything at all on their own because they're afraid of making a mistake. They always try to shove the blame off on someone else. You'll find that accepting the responsibility for your own actions and for the actions of your subordinates ties in quite closely with moral courage.

Wise men admit their mistakes.

"One of the best signs that you're growing up is when you're willing to accept the responsibility of your own mistakes," Dr. Wayne Morrow, head of the psychology department at Simpson College told me. "It takes both courage and wisdom to admit your mistakes, especially when they're very stupid and very foolish.

"I make mistakes every day of the week, and I suppose I'll keep on doing so the rest of my life. I try not to make the same one twice in the same day, but even that's too hard for me most of the time.

"But I console myself every time I see a pencil. I figure that if people didn't make mistakes, they'd soon stop making pencils with erasers."

12. Assuming the responsibility for what you fail to do is just as important as assuming the responsibility for what you do.

Not doing it is no excuse.

Assumption of responsibility covers not only what you do, it also includes *taking the responsibility for what you fail to do.*

Just being good isn't going to get you into Heaven. You've got to do more than that; you've got to do some good if you want to go knocking on those pearly gates.

Remember that the leader or the executive who truly accepts his responsibility in the fullest sense will be responsible, not only for what his organization does but also for what it fails to do.

13. In the absence of any standing orders, seize the initiative and take the action you believe that your superior would direct you to take if he were present.

Do what you think is right.

If you don't seize the initiative and take some kind of action, remember that someone else will, if not at that time, the next time for sure. He'll have replaced you by then.

The only requirement here is that the action you take be in line with your superior's previously established policy. In other words, do what you think is the right thing to do.

As General Charles C. Curran used to tell his brigade officers, "Do something, even if it's wrong; but do something! Don't just stand there."

To Sum It All Up

Actively seek responsibility and you'll develop yourself professionally. Taking the initiative in the absence of orders from your superior is one of the primary signs that you've learned to accept responsibility.

When you take the responsibility for your own actions and for the actions of your subordinates, you'll gain their respect and their confidence. They'll give you their willing obedience, their loyal cooperation, and their full support.

Don't be afraid of making mistakes. There's a big difference between mistakes and failures. Mistakes can be forgiven; failures cannot. You must still accept your responsibility even after you've reached the top. You'll never be able to abdicate it and stay up there.

Recapitulation of the Thirteen Keys for Application of the Ninth Dynamic Law of Motivation

1. *You must learn your profession from the ground up while you are developing your capacity for accepting heavy responsibilities in the future.*
2. *Learn the duties of your immediate superior thoroughly, and be prepared to accept his responsibilities on a moment's notice.*
3. *You must be physically, mentally, and psychologically qualified to shoulder heavy responsibilities.*
4. *Always seek diversified management assignments so you can gain and develop a broad experience in the acceptance of responsibility.*
5. *Take full advantage of every opportunity that offers you an increased responsibility.*
6. *Perform every task, large or small, to the best of your ability.*
7. *Accept just and honest criticism and admit your mistakes.*
8. *Stick to what you think is right; have the courage of your convictions.*
9. *You must assume full responsibility for the failures of those who work for you.*
10. *Carefully study, analyze, and evaluate a subordinate's failure before taking any corrective action.*
11. *You must assume complete responsibility for your own actions.*
12. *Assuming the responsibility for what you fail to do is just as important as assuming the responsibility for what you do.*
13. *In the absence of any standing orders, seize the initiative and take the action you believe that your superior would direct you to take if he were present.*

Dynamic Law #10

Always
Set the Example

Always set the example so your men can use you and your actions to determine their own standards of conduct and efficiency.

Always set the example so you'll be able to motivate your men to do as you do. The attitudes, the actions, and the reactions of the people who work for you will be deeply influenced by the personal qualities you have and the example that you set for them. Everyone tends to do as his superior does, so set the proper example for your men to follow, and you'll be able to motivate them to do the same as you do.

Your individual appearance and conduct must be such that they'll bring forth from your subordinates respect and pride, and they'll be motivated with a desire to meet your standards.

The people who work for you will always use your weaknesses and your shortcomings as excuses for their own failures and their own wrongdoings. The qualities you have, either bad or good, and your actions, too, will directly influence their behavior, and therefore, what they will or will not do for you. Your individual appearance must be so meticulous and your conduct so proper that you'll always motivate them to do the right thing.

164

> *Always set the standard for your entire organization by your out-standing performance of duty, and you'll motivate your employees to reach that same high peak of perfection.*

If you'll just follow the maxim of the South's great hero, Robert E. Lee, you'll never go wrong. He said, "Do your duty in all things. You could not do more. You would not wish to do less." Follow this principle and you'll always motivate your employees to do the same.

> *The whole purpose of the motivation of others is to inspire each one of them to give forth with his best efforts possible in line with his own individual abilites. Always set the example and you'll be close to achieving your goal.*

Always set the example, and you'll be able to gain the respect, the confidence, the willing obedience, the loyal cooperation, and the full support of all your employees. You'll be able to motivate them to do their utmost for you.

How It Works

There are only six specific techniques I'm going to give to you which will make this dynamic law of motivation—always set the example—work for you. There are others, perhaps, but if you can achieve perfection in these six, you'll never need worry about yourself as an example any more.

Use them, apply them daily, and you'll soon be able to develop these personal qualities to the point that your own employees will want to follow your example. You'll motivate them to do their best for you, and you'll be able to get them to do what you want them to do.

Remember that leaders are examples to be followed, not models to be admired. Setting the example isn't going to be an easy task. It means you're going to have to develop or strengthen some of those old-fashioned personal qualities you and I used to hear about in Sunday-School when we were children.

Setting the example means developing such personal traits as courage, integrity, tact, unselfishness, dependability, and a host of others. Setting the example means sticking to what you know to be morally right even when it would be so much easier not to do so. What's the old saying? Everything I like to do is illegal, immoral, or fattening.

But as Albert Schweitzer said, "Example is not the main thing in life, it is the only thing." So set the proper example and you'll not need to preach a sermon to your men. They'll need only to follow in your footsteps to do the right thing.

For your men will always look to you as the example for them to follow. If you set a poor example for them, in no matter what way, they'll always use you as an excuse for their own mistakes and their own shortcomings. If a man can't climb up to your level, he'll always try to drag you down to his.

By your own individual appearance and your own exemplary conduct you must bring forth from your men respect for you, pride in you, and a strong desire to live up to your standards.

You must set that standard for your entire group by your own outstanding performance of duty. There is no compromise.

The Six Keys for Application of the Tenth Dynamic Law of Motivation

Always set the example.

1. *You must be at all times physically fit, mentally alert, morally correct, well-groomed, and properly dressed.*

2. *You must learn to master your emotions completely.*

3. *Always keep a cheerful and an optimistic outlook and attitude.*

4. *Conduct yourself at all times so that your personal habits will not be open to criticism or censure from anyone.*

5. *To set the example, you must always use tact and courtesy.*

6. *Your word must be your bond.*

Discussion of the Six Keys for Application of the Tenth Dynamic Law of Motivation

1. You must be at all times physically fit, mentally alert, morally correct, well-groomed, and properly dressed.

You must be physically fit and mentally alert.

Endurance, the ability to stick to the task no matter what happens, will be a personal quality you'll have to develop to apply this first key in your daily activities.

Actually, endurance is closely tied in with courage. It is that staying power you need when things are really rough. It's the ability to run the mile as well as the hundred yard dash. Endurance can also be thought of as that physical and mental stamina that's required to withstand the stress of pain, fatigue, hardship, and even verbal criticism.

Endurance is your ability to perform successfully under extreme mental and physical strain for long periods of time. It's that extra effort you'll need for the long haul. It's your second wind. And it's an important trait of motivation you'll need if you want to gain the proper respect from your subordinates.

Endurance and courage are comparable.

"Often a lack of endurance can be confused with a lack of courage," Bill Bayless, the football coach of Glendale High School in Springfield, Missouri, told me. "You need physical stamina as well as mental stamina to develop the endurance it takes for high school football. Sometimes, a fellow can be mistakenly taken for a coward and a weakling simply because of his poor physical condition."

True enough, some of you might not need endurance in a physical way as much as others do. But whether you do or not, I will say this. Lots of adrenalin and glucose will be needed to stick to a given task and see it through to a successful conclusion, no matter what obstacles you run into.

To develop your mental and physical endurance, practice following these five guidelines daily.

(1) *Stay away from activities that tend to lower your physical efficiency.*

Too much smoking will cut your wind, if nothing more. Science seems to think it'll do more. Too much alcohol will lower your body resistance. It'll decrease your ability to think clearly. In the end, it could result in drastic physical and mental changes, and all for the worse.

Few, if any, drunkards have ever become successful managers or executives. Many successful ones have been toppled from their high positions of authority and responsibility by becoming alcohol-dependent. I'm not beating any drum for total abstinence here. I'm simply stating facts. What you do about it is entirely up to you.

But you'll never be able to think clearly and properly when your physical stamina, your health, and your well-being are not completely normal, no matter whether it's due to alcohol or to some other cause. Try making a sound and timely decision when you're sick or, say, after the fifth or sixth martini.

(2) *Develop physical training habits that will strengthen your body.*

Isometric exercises seem to be the latest thing for those of us who are chained to a desk. But no matter what kind of physical exercise you use to keep fit, try to build up your endurance by using the *overload principle.*

The overload principle is simply the proven scientific fact that muscular development and improvement depend upon the demand you impose on your muscles. *The demand must increase as your ability increases if you expect improvement to continue.*

(3) *Learn a sport you can play by yourself and still enjoy it when you grow older.*

Baseball, tennis, volleyball—all these are wonderful group sports when you're young enough to take it. Golf, bowling, hunting, fishing are sports you can enjoy with others as well as by yourself. Personally, I like bowling better than golf; someone always throws my ball back to me.

(4) *Test your mental endurance by frequently forcing yourself to do strenuous mental work.*

Push yourself to work sometimes at mental tasks when you're deathly tired and your mind is sluggish and worn out. It's the only way you'll ever learn to operate under real pressure. This again is using the *overload principle.*

(5) *Finish every job you've been given to the best of your physical and mental abilities.*

This is usually the best test of your endurance. It's the one that takes the courage as well as the endurance.

You'll need to develop bearing and poise too.

The dictionary defines bearing as the way you carry and conduct yourself. It's your way of standing or sitting or walking. It's your manner and your demeanor; your carriage and your poise.

Bearing is also that favorable first impression.

Bearing is also the way you dress, the way you look, the way you talk. You might describe it as that *favorable first impression* you've got to make. And you might as well make that first impression as good as you can, for in most cases, it's the lasting one.

When you do have the proper bearing, it means you'll create that good and favorable impression on others by your poise, your appearance, your conduct, not only at first, but always.

Good or bad, your bearing will set the standard which your superiors, your subordinates, your associates, and your friends will use to judge you. And your men will always tend to follow the example you've set for them when they set their own standards of right or wrong conduct.

Bearing includes your posture.

Your posture should always be upright; you can't create a favorable impression on others if you slump and drag around. Do that, and you become at once the picture of dejection and discouragement. Don't look like a pessimist; you'll soon be one.

To keep an upright posture, always think tall, sit tall, stand tall. I don't care what your height is. It matters not if you're 5 feet 6 or 6 feet 5. Remember Napoleon? He might've been short, but he made all the history books and encyclopedias. Height has nothing to do with creating an upright appearance.

Right here I want to give you four guidelines you can use daily to help you develop good bearing:

(1) *Always discipline yourself.*

Always keep yourself under control. Conduct yourself at all times according to the highest acceptable social standards in both your appearance and conduct.

(2) *Don't use vulgar and obscene language.*

Avoid coarse and rude behavior and the use of vulgar and obscene language. Remember that you're supposed to be setting the example, so be the perfect gentleman at all times.

(3) *Drink only in moderation.*

If you drink, do so only in moderation. Never drink with your subordinates and never let them see you drunk.

(4) *Always maintain a dignified manner.* However, don't think this means that you have to make yourself unapproachable.

You are always on display.

You must also set the example for your subordinates to follow by your general appearance, your personal cleanliness, the neatness and the general condition of your clothing.

So be alert! Follow the Gillette slogan: Look sharp, feel sharp, be sharp! You must radiate alertness, confidence, and dynamic energy. Motivate your men by your dynamic appearance and actions. Remember that as an executive, a manager, a supervisor, a leader, *you are always on display!*

2. You must learn to master your emotions completely.

Instead of flying off into a great rage, fly off into a great calm.

"A man is just as big as the things that made him mad," Guy Fowler, a retired restaurant owner from Webster City, Iowa, told me. "And in the restaurant business, there are a lot of things that could get you down if you'd let them.

"I always tried to keep two things in mind when I was in business. One was this: *Never let someone else's inferiority overcome your superiority.* The other was, when things go wrong, *instead of flying off into a great rage, fly off into a great calm.*"

You must always be consistent.

If you're subject to uncontrollable bursts of temper, or to deep periods of depression, you'll have great difficulty in gaining and holding the respect and loyalty of your subordinates. They'll never know for sure what your reactions are going to be when they bring problems to you. As their superior, you must always be consistent.

If you can't control yourself, you can't control others.

If you do happen to have a tendency to be easily irritated by small things, if by nature you somehow seem to have been given a sour disposition (most people are pessimistic, you know), if you display frequent temper tantrums as a spoiled child will, then I'll say to you right now: Get rid of those bad habits!

It isn't just a matter of getting people to like you, although that's important too. It's really a matter of getting them to work for you, to do what you want them to do, to put out their best efforts for you.

If you let your temper and a sour disposition creep in, it will simply show them that you lack self-discipline and self-control. They'll know you can never be depended upon to do the right thing in an emergency.

A loss of temper usually indicates that you don't have complete confidence in yourself and in your own abilities. You're probably running scared of the boss or scared of losing your job. At any rate, you'd best remember that if you can't control yourself, you'll never begin to control others.

Don't be harsh when handling people.

Never be too harsh, too firm, or too severe in your manner of handling your subordinates. If you allow anger or prejudice to creep into your decisions and into your management, you'll never be able to gain their respect, their confidence, their willing obedience and loyal cooperation. And without these, you'll never have their full support.

Without their full support, how can you possibly motivate them to do the things you want them to do? So never let your emotions of anger or prejudice creep into your decisions or into your methods of supervising your men. Heart? Yes. Emotions? Never!

Make the extra-special effort.

"I've always made an extra-special effort never to let any of my personal problems enter my work," Frank Foster, head of the Social Security Office in Kansas City, Missouri, told me.

"I don't care how upset I've been with my wife or my children or the monthly bills, I've always tried never to carry those troubles to the office. Oh, maybe I've missed the boat once in a while, but for the most part, I've never let those underlying emotions come to the surface.

"You see, before I ever get out of my car in the morning to go into the office, I always stop long enough to crank a smile on my face, no matter what I feel like inside. And it pays me dividends, too.

"More than once I've had some of my office personnel say to me, 'Frank, it's really a pleasure to work for you. You're so consistent, and that's really important the first thing in the morning. You always come in with a big grin and a cheerful "Good morning!" for everyone.'

"You know, Jim," Frank went on, "it really is miserable to work for someone who comes to work with a big grouch every morning. You just never know which way to jump, except to get back out of the way. Before I took over the office, we had a boss who was just like that.

"So remembering him and how everybody disliked him and feared him so much, I've always made an extra-special effort to *greet 'em with a smile and send 'em home with a smile!* Oh, we might have a few rough spots in between, but we try to start her off right and finish her up right anyway."

Don't swear or yell at your men.

Foul, rotten language in a loud tone of voice will never get the results you want or expect to get. If you always use profanity and obscene language, then don't expect anything different at all from your men. They'll automatically mimic your style, your mannerisms, and your vocabulary, and soon it will be their own.

If you permit your subordinate supervisors to constantly swear, especially when they're giving out their orders, you're really asking for trouble. Men naturally and rightfully resent being cursed out by anyone, but especially their superiors, for they feel there's little they can do about it.

I feel that way, and I'm sure you do too. Whenever you curse out a man who works for you, you're taking an unfair advantage of your position, and you're using your authority in a way you're not entitled to. A tongue lashing will always be thought of as a personal attack by the person on the receiving end.

If you must criticize and correct others in your capacity, make sure your criticism is helpful and constructive. Never let your emotions enter the picture when you're correcting someone. The moment you become angry in your attempt to correct someone's actions the issue becomes cloudy and obscure. The end result will be nothing more than a personal argument, usually a shouting match, between two people.

If ever there's a time for violent language . . .

If ever there's a time or an excuse for the use of violent language and harsh words, then it could be only during an extreme physical emergency of some sort when someone is physically in danger. It might be that a verbal tongue lashing or a fiery tongue at that time could be of some value, but I doubt it.

If it does have any value at all at such a time, it would only be if the effect of such language would be to stimulate or somehow steady the actions of a certain individual. But if you use this kind of language all the time, then the effects of it would be completely lost just at the moment when you really need it.

"I've learned a few things in my life of working with others, and one thing I have learned is this," Ronald Stewart, the director of industrial relations for the Yates Tool and Die Company out in Wichita, Kansas, told me.

"Never yell at a man unless he's so far away you have to shout to make him hear you!

"Shouting or yelling at a man at any other time has no value whatever that I can see. It only creates trouble."

3. Always keep a cheerful and an optimistic outlook and attitude.

Who wants to back a loser anyway?

The will to win is contagious. Develop this will-to-win-attitude in your men by making the most of your organization's successes.

But no matter how things are going, you must always show an attitude of calmness and confidence and quiet optimism at all times. And the more difficult the situation, the more important this will become.

With energy and enthusiasm, a bad decision can often be brought to a successful conclusion.

Since you're always on display, you'll have to show confidence and competence in your manner and in your actions, often far beyond what you may actually feel.

But by properly controlling your voice, your gestures, your mannerisms, you'll be able to exert a strong, a powerful, and a steadying influence on those around you even when you're not feeling your best.

Every successful person knows that just as long as he shows an apparent and natural confidence in both himself and his subordinates, a bad decision can often be carried on through to a successful conclusion. Many a battle has been won against overwhelming odds by the confidence of men in their leaders.

Sarcasm and irony are not optimism and cheerfulness.

Sarcasm and irony will never get the results you want from your men. First of all, most people, and that includes me, too, do not understand sarcasm and irony; and secondly, no one enjoys a joke that's at his own expense.

You just can't expect to get along well with people if you're going to poke *so-called* fun at them all the time and make them the butt of every joke. They'll always resent you for that.

If you want to use jokes to illustrate your point or to make an example, fine, do so; but tell your jokes Jack Benny style. In other words, make yourself the goat or the butt of your jokes.

Most Americans do hear this bantering and joking kind of talk all the time. They're so accustomed to sarcastic jokes at their expense, they can't resist answering back in the same way, as long as they feel safe and secure in doing so.

If your men are constantly on the receiving end of sarcasm and irony and practical jokes, they'll have a good reason to feel that they, too, can respond in exactly the same manner to you. You'll have no respect from them whatever.

There'll be times, of course, when you'll really need that jovial and cheerful manner even if you have to force it. When your men are discouraged or tired, when there's trouble brewing, when their working conditions are bad, then a spot of humor and a good laugh can help to relieve the tension and the strain of the bad situation.

In fact, we often look at this as our American way of showing sympathy, understanding, friendship, and cooperation in the midst of great difficulty. Just make sure you know the difference between a cheerful optimistic attitude and useless sarcasm and irony.

4. Conduct yourself at all times so that your personal habits will not be open to criticism or censure from anyone.

Watch your language—everyone else will.

Another one of the critical outward signs in setting the example is your language and your choice of words. I've made reference to swearing before. Right now I have another thought in mind. Your men will always watch you closely for any mistakes. If they notice a mistake in your pronunciation, your grammer, or your vocabulary, you'll have slipped a notch or so in their estimation of you.

Oh, they might make that same mistake a dozen times a day, but that's not the same at all. It's an odd thing with employees; they love to catch their boss in any mistake, no matter how small that mistake is. It immediately makes them feel so superior to their boss.

And your superiors will also watch for such mistakes, and in a way perhaps, this is even more important, especially when the time comes for your promotion to a higher position of responsibility and authority. Watch your language, and you'll have motivated them properly.

The goal of effective communication is to be understood.

Of course, the real goal of effective communication is to make yourself understood so there'll be no possibility of a mistake or the slightest chance of a misunderstanding.

But you can make yourself understood just as well with proper English and correct grammar as well as with the language of the gutter. Why open the door to criticism when just a bit of caution and care on your part will keep it tightly closed for you.

You don't have to use poor pronunciation, sloppy grammar, and a choice of vulgar words to make yourself understood. Usually these show nothing more than pure laziness and a complete lack of self-discipline on your part. Many times, your superiors will look at it as simply a lack of good breeding.

Oh, I don't mean you have to be an absolute master of college or even high school English and grammar, but an honest effort on your part will pay off for you in the long run with both your subordinates and your superiors.

Use simple words.

"The longer I teach the English language, I find that simple words are much better to use," Dr. Arthur Malone, head of the English department at Drury College in Springfield, Missouri, told me.

"You see, they're much safer to use than a shower of flowery adjectives which are used only in a vain attempt to impress others.

The beauty of using a small word is that you know exactly what it means at first sight, and people understand you immediately."

I must agree whole-heartedly with Dr. Malone. Trying to use big words to impress others is a waste of time. You'll be fooling no one but yourself; people will see through you immediately.

So when you speak to others, speak plainly and clearly. Make your sentences short, simple, positive, direct and to the point.

If you do use big words, explain their use.

If you must use words and terms that might not be clearly understood, even by only one person, simply make sure they're needed and that they cannot be replaced by simpler ones.

If you must then use them, do so; but when you do, make sure you explain their actual meanings and show exactly how you're using them. Do that, and you can be sure your men will always understand what you want from them.

Don't use those big words just to impress people.

Don't ever use big words to talk down to your subordinates trying to impress them with your vast store of knowledge. You'll be laughed at, resented, or both.

People used to feel that a big vocabulary of rarely used words would somehow automatically guarantee success. Not any more. That kind of thinking is old-fashioned. The only real advantage you'll ever find for an extensive vocabulary is that *it's far better for catching than it is for pitching*.

Just for example now, here's a perfectly correct sentence, at least, as far as the grammar goes: *Simians indigenous to Zamboanga are destitute of caudal appendages*. Sounds very impressive, doesn't it? All it means is that *monkeys have no tails in Zamboanga*.

Try this system.

On my desk is a card which I use for guidance in my choice of words. It says:

"If you're tempted to use a big word just to show off your knowledge and your education and to show just how smart you are, *don't do it!*

"But if you honestly feel that big word is the only one that will say exactly what you want to say and that no other word will say it quite as well, then for heaven's sake *use it!*"

You must be dignified!

To set the example, to have an excellent bearing, you must always be dignified. Many people seem to think that dignity is reserved only for ministers and undertakers. They feel that dignity means that you must have a sad, long face, always wear a black funeral coat and tie, and never get any fun out of life at all.

Well, between us, I don't think that's dignity at all. Some people might call it solemnity, but it's surely not dignity.

Dignity, first of all, means a state of being worthy and honorable. It means that one possesses complete control over all his emotions and his actions at all times.

For instance, the supervisor who makes a complete fool out of himself through loud and boisterous talk, obscene jokes and vulgar language, excessive drinking, or the complete loss of his emotional control in fits of anger is surely not dignified at all.

He's nothing but a complete fool. He'll immediately lose the respect of his men. He's not meant to be a supervisor, an executive, or a manager, and he won't be up there long at all. *Once you've lost the respect of your men, it's almost impossible to regain it!*

Everyone tends to do as his superior does.

The attitudes, the actions, and the reactions of the people who work for you will be deeply influenced by the personal qualities you have. *Everyone tends to do as his superior does,* not only in his strong points, *but especially in his weak ones!*

The people who work for you will always use your weaknesses and your shortcomings as an excuse for their own failures and their own mistakes. The qualities you have, either bad or good, and your actions, too, will directly influence their behavior and, therefore, what they will or will not do for you.

Don't get caught riding in the wheelbarrow.

How your subordinates will always use the weaknesses of the boss to justify their own actions is shown in this little story I want to tell you right now.

It was during a seasonal office party—you know the kind I mean, I'm sure, the kind where we all let our hair down, and let bygones be bygones—that one of the employees drank a bit more than was actually good for him.

In fact, he was just barely able to remember what had happened during the party; afterward was even more hazy. And some things he wanted to forget, anyway. But not everyone wanted to forget what he'd done, evidently; for the day after that party, he was told to report to the president's office.

"John," said the president to the shaky one, "I'm truly sorry, but after what you did yesterday, well, I have no choice; I'm forced to let you go.

"You see, I heard that after the party broke up you were seen pushing a wheelbarrow down the middle of Main Street, interfering with traffic, and in short, making a complete fool of yourself. I didn't see it myself, but that's the way the report has come back to me.

"John, that's just too far. I know it was a party, and all that, but after all, we can't have one of our top men in the company doing a thing like that, now can we? That's too much; you've pushed me over the line, John. People do talk, you know. Can't stand for that. Not good for the fine name and reputation of my company. Sorry."

John looked at his boss for a moment or so in open-mouthed astonishment. Then he said, "Boss, I just can't understand your attitude at all. I don't see why you should object to my pushing a wheelbarrow down the street. After all, you were the one getting the free ride!"

5. To set the example, you must always use tact and courtesy.

What is tact anyway?

Tact is that ability to say or do the right thing at the right time without offending anyone. It will take a lot of skill and tact

when you're dealing with difficult persons or with touchy situations. You must always have a quick and delicate sense of just
what is best fitting to the occasion.

To be tactful, you must have a good understanding of human
nature and a sympathetic consideration for the feelings of others.
Tact will be important to you in all your personal relationships
with your superiors, your subordinates, and your associates.

I look at tact this way. It is that capability you must have to
say or do whatever is necessary to accomplish your mission, but
without giving any unnecessary offense to anyone, or at the expense of a single person's welfare.

Courtesy is a part of tact.

Courtesy can also be considered as a part of tact. You simply
cannot afford to be discourteous in your relationships with either
your superiors or your subordinates. No, not even your associates.

If you demand courtesy, but you fail to return it in full measure, you show only arrogance, a lack of interest in others, no
breeding, or as many of us might say—he's simply had no
fetchin' up!

Seven ways to develop tact and courtesy.

(1) *Always be cheerful and optimistic in your manner.*

(2) *Be considerate of others in everything you do; always think of the other fellow's feelings.*

(3) *Study the methods of those who've already gained
a reputation for being skilled in the art of human relations.*

(4) *Cooperate in spirit as well as in fact.*

Don't live just the letter of the law alone; get some heart
and some feeling into it, too.

(5) *Maintain a tolerant attitude toward others; live and
let live.*

(6) *Don't criticize or talk about others.*

But for the grace of God, there go I. Never criticize
where another fellow walks unless you've worn his shoes.
Treat others with the same kind consideration you want for
yourself.

(7) *Know when your presence is required, both offi-cially and socially.*

Be tactful enough to find out if your presence is either desired or required. If not, leave immediately and gracefully.

6. Your word must be your bond.

Always make your word good.

If you're going to be a top-level executive, you must be as good as your word and your word must be your bond. To make sure that you can always keep your word, keep these three points always in mind:

(1) *Never make a promise that you cannot keep.*

(2) *Never make a decision that you cannot support.*

(3) *Never issue an order that you cannot enforce.*

Personal integrity is a must.

If you don't possess this personal quality of integrity, you'll never be able to set the example. In fact, without it, everything else you might do to motivate your men will be completely useless. Without a sense of personal integrity you might as well quit. If you're a liar, how could you possibly motivate anyone?

Integrity is that quality or state of being of sound moral principle. It stands for uprightness of character, absolute truthfulness, candid honesty, and deep sincerity. *It is an absolute must!*

There can be no middle ground here whatever; there can be no compromise. Your slightest deviation from the highest possible standards of personal integrity will destroy you as far as becoming a top-notch executive.

If you're a liar, you simply cannot be depended upon in any way; you cannot be relied upon. You could be a genius, yet as an executive you'd be completely worthless. Unless you're capable of being honest, you might as well forget about using the other dynamics of motivation to get people to do their best for you. They won't!

Let me give you five guidelines you can follow to help you develop high standards of personal integrity.

(1) *Practice absolute honesty and truthfulness in everything at all times.*

Don't allow yourself the luxury of even one tiny white lie.

(2) *Be accurate and correct in everything you say and do.*

(3) *Your signature on any document is a certification as to the truthfulness of that document.*

When you write a personal check, your signature is a certificate to the effect that you have money in that bank. Your signature in your work and in your business must carry exactly that same weight.

(4) *Stand for what you believe to be right.*

Have the courage of your convictions, regardless of the consequences. Never compromise your standards; never prostitute your principles.

(5) *Duty and honor come first.*

If ever you're tempted to compromise your principles, then you must place honesty and your sense of duty and personal honor above all else.

If you can grasp, understand, and practice the ideas of duty and honor, you cannot help but develop personal integrity.

To Sum It All Up

Only by setting the example can the image of the leader be created. If you want to succeed, to be a successful executive or manager, you must always set the example.

Your personality will have a far reaching effect and influence upon your employees. In fact, the personality and the attitude of the organization is simply an extension of your own individual personality.

If you appear in an unfavorable light before your men, you'll destroy the mutual confidence and respect that must exist between you and your men.

In short, to set the example does not mean to do as I say, it means to *do as I do!*

Recapitulation of the Six Keys for Application of the Tenth Dynamic Law of Motivation

1. *You must be at all times physically fit, mentally alert, morally correct, well-groomed, and properly dressed.*
2. *You must learn to master your emotions completely.*
3. *Always keep a cheerful and an optimistic outlook and attitude.*
4. *Conduct yourself at all times so that your personal habits will not be open to criticism or censure from anyone.*
5. *To set the example, you must always use tact and courtesy.*
6. *Your word must be your bond.*

Dynamic Law #11

Motivate Every Single Man to Feel Important to Himself

Motivate a man to feel important to himself, and you'll win his heart as well as his head.

If you'll make a man and his work important, not only to you and your organization, but primarily to himself, and always be hearty in your praise of him, you'll find that you can motivate him to want to do what you want him to do. And to properly motivate a man to do what you want him to do, you must win his heart before you win his head. Whatever you want might be logical enough, but unless you can make a man want it enough, you'll simply not get the job done. Remember that the only way to get a man to do what you want him to do is for him to want to do it first.

The Apostle Paul, the greatest salesman Christianity has ever had, didn't sell the doctrines of Christ on logic alone. He had to win the hearts of the people first: the head never hears 'til the heart has listened.

Make a man important to himself by letting him know that he's both wanted and needed, and he'll go all out to help you achieve your own goals.

When a man knows that he's really wanted and that his efforts are truly appreciated, when he feels that he's contributing something worthwhile to the achievement of a common goal, you've made that man feel important to himself; and he'll go all out to get the job done for you. He'll be proud of himself, proud of those who work with him, and he'll be proud of you and the organization as a whole.

Make a man important to himself by giving him your sincere appreciation and thanks and you'll motivate him to give you his full support.

Your appreciation must be genuine and sincere. Flattery will get you nowhere. Your men will see through you at once. Flattery is as phony as a three-dollar bill. If you want to get a man's full support by motivating him to feel important to himself, you must really mean it when you pay him a compliment.

How It Works

You'll find there are thirteen precise methods of application which will make this dynamic law of motivation—the motivation of every single man *to feel important to himself*—work for you. Each one of them, properly applied, will help you win the hearts of your employees.

Motivating every single man to look at himself with respect and pride and getting each one to do what you want him to do, and not what he wants to do, is truly an art. It's a dynamic and moving art. The motivation of people to do what you want them to do—winning their hearts—is an art, and not a precise science.

What's the difference between a science and an art? Well, a science deals with things, and therefore, it's quite predictable. But an art deals with people, and as a result, it's quite unpredictable for the simple reason that people are also quite unpredictable, too.

That's why medicine can be a science in the laboratory, but an art in the doctor's office. When the druggist fills the doctor's prescription, that's a science. When the doctor prescribes the medicine for the patient's prescription in his office, that's an art.

You could also say that an art is the language of the heart; a science the language of the head. And even though this dynamic law of motivation—make every single man feel important to himself—is an art by definition, it's also scientifically correct. *It's been proven in the biggest laboratory of all, life itself!*

Most psychologists will insist that you must make a man important to you, but the key to it is this: *You must first make that man important to himself.* Once he feels important to himself, once he feels a strong sense of self-pride and self-respect, when he loves himself, then you make him feel important to you.

Jesus taught the same principle when he said, "Thou shalt love thy neighbor as thyself." But most people forget the last two words of this quotation, *as thyself.* For a clearer understanding of this principle, try substituting the words *respect* and *honor* for the word *love* in this quotation of Christ's.

Making another man important to himself is one of the biggest secrets of success of some of the richest and most famous people throughout history. Use this principle, and I can guarantee you'll be successful, too. You'll be able to get what you want to get out of life, and that's really what success is, isn't it?

The Thirteen Keys for Application of the Eleventh Dynamic Law of Motivation

Motivate every single man to feel important to himself.

1. *You'll motivate a man to feel important to himself when you appeal to his heart and not his head!*
2. *Motivate a man to feel important to himself by becoming genuinely interested in him and in what he does.*
3. *Make a man feel important to himself by talking in terms of his interests.*
4. *Always remember a man's name; it's the most important word in all the world to him.*
5. *Motivate a man to feel important to himself by giving him individual identity in your organization.*
6. *A man will feel important to himself, to you and to your*

    organization if you use him primarily in the job for which he's been trained.

7. *Motivate a man to feel important to himself by giving him a personal need and a desire to learn.*
8. *Give a man a sense of self-importance by keeping him well-informed about his individual progress in your organization.*
9. *Motivate a man to feel important to himself by rewarding his successes gained through competition with his associates.*
10. *Make a man feel important to himself by asking for his advice and help.*
11. *Motivate a man to feel self-important by allowing him to set his own goals in his own job.*
12. *Let a man develop a sense of importance by showing him how essential his efforts are and where he fits into the big picture.*
13. *You can make every man feel important to himself if you'll just put PERSONAL into PERSONNEL!*

Discussion of the Thirteen Keys for Application of the Eleventh Dynamic Law of Motivation

1. You'll motivate a man to feel important to himself when you appeal to his heart and not his head!

How to get a mink coat.

Tell me now, does your wife have a mink coat or a mink stole? And how did she get it please? By appealing to your heart or to your head? Let me tell you how my wife got hers. True enough, she might have used a little head, but she used heart first, cold hard logic last.

One warm spring night she met me at the door wearing a low-cut provocative dress. There was a smile on her lips, stars in her eyes, apples in her cheeks, perfume on her ear and a promise of better things yet to come in her kiss.

I could sniff the faint but definite smell of porterhouse steaks broiling in the charcoal oven. My subconscious rang an alarm bell of warning, but it was a waste of time.

After dinner was over, and I'd settled down in my favorite chair with my pipe and slippers, brought to me by my adoring wife, of course, she laid the evening paper in my lap, all apologies for having gotten some of the pages mixed up.

I'll say they were mixed up! She'd handed me a paper, part of which had been published in early September of last year, and part of which had been published today in late May.

And two pages of fur advertisements had been carefully placed side by side. One page from the September paper showed the offerings of the Jones Store's fall fur sale; the other from the current one showed the bargains to be had in the present spring fur sale.

How well I remembered that my wife had wanted a mink last fall. And I also remembered that I'd put her off with the idea that the prices were outrageous, we couldn't afford it right then; and there was some sort of a vague promise about getting her one in the spring when the prices would be oh-so-much lower, now wouldn't they, dear?

So what do you think? Did she get her mink? With a hat yet to match!

Appeal to a man's heart and you'll improve his morale.

Morale is that mood and the spirit that makes a man want to do a decent job for you. A man who has high morale is not only willing to work, he wants you to depend on him to do an outstanding job.

A man's morale is based on many factors, true enough, but primarily it springs from his faith in the cause, the program, his work, the organization, and his confidence in his superiors, his leaders.

Morale is a matter of mind, not matter.

In its simplest terms, morale—no matter whether it's high or low—means the state of mind of the individual. This individual state of mind depends upon a man's attitude toward everything that affects him, directly or indirectly: his fellow workers, his superiors, the organization as a whole, his life in general, his outside activities, and on and on and on.

Morale is primarily dependent, however, upon a man satisfying his emotional needs and wants. If your organization is geared toward helping your men satisfy those basic needs and wants, then a favorable attitude toward life in general, toward you and your organization, will be developed in them.

High morale among your men and a positive mental outlook will give them a feeling of confidence, security, and well-being. They'll work for you with endurance, determination, enthusiasm, and ambition.

2. Motivate a man to feel important to himself by becoming genuinely interested in him and in what he does.

This takes some effort on your part.

If you want to motivate a man by becoming genuinely interested in him and in what he does, you must have a positive, sincere, and friendly attitude toward others. You must have or you must develop an out-going personality.

You'll have to learn to work in close association with others and to get along with them, giving your full attention to their interests. Always develop the big *YOU* and the little *i* to make it work.

Jerry Jackson makes it work.

Jerry Jackson, a department head in the Brown Shoe Company in Memphis, Tennessee, was having a tough time getting his men to respond to his orders and his directives. He was getting no cooperation whatever from them. In fact, most of the time his men were surly, stubborn, and completely indifferent about getting the job done. Yet Jerry knew as much about the shoe manufacturing business as anyone in the plant.

His problem? All too simple, really. You see, Jerry hadn't learned yet that *executives work with people, not with things.*

Jerry always made it a practice to walk through his department each morning to see how the work was going. He'd walk up to a piece of machinery, check it, and then say to the group of men standing there in an off-hand manner, "Mornin', fellas."

But I noticed that his eyes were focused only on the machinery and its product, never on the men themselves. Nor would he wait for an answering "Good morning" from his men, but he would immediately launch into what he termed his *orders for the day.*

"Jerry, why do you even say 'Good morning' to your men," I asked him.

"Got to," he said. "If you don't, they'll think you're a stuck-up snob. I always say 'Good morning' to my men. Good practice. Improves management-labor relations, they tell me."

"Then why don't you look them in the eye?" I asked him. "And why don't you call them by their first names? They are human beings, Jerry. They're real live people. They're not cattle or sticks of wood or chunks of stone, you know. And they're a lot more important to you than those machines you look at when you go through your department each morning.

"Why don't you call each man by his first name when you say 'Good morning' to him, and for a change, look him straight in the eye when you say it. And let him know that you really do mean a *good*-good morning to him.

"Or why don't you surprise him a little more? Ask him how he is. Or how the wife and the kids are getting along. How's Johnny doing in the army, that sort of thing.

"And then, Jerry, you'd better get back out of the way. He'll be producing 150 percent for you if you don't watch out. He might even get you promoted to be president of your company!"

A few days later Jerry called me. "It works! It works!" he yelled in my ear. "Why, it's like magic. The men really do like me, and they're working like I've never seen them work before. And all I did was call them by their first names and show a little interest in them."

3. Make a man feel important to himself by talking in terms of his interests.

Offer a man opportunity for promotion and advancement.

Any man is always interested in financial reward. Talk to him in these terms and you can be sure you're talking about something he's deeply interested in. Who doesn't like money? But by the same token, money isn't always enough.

Of course, if you pay a man a decent salary to begin with, and if you always keep the possibility of a pay raise or a promotion in front of his eyes, you're not only talking in terms of his interests, you're fulfilling one of his basic needs.

But money is a *need* only up to a certain point; after that point is reached then money becomes a *want*. You cannot dangle the *need* part of a man's salary in front of his nose and expect to get the desired results. He'll simply leave you and go to work somewhere else where he is paid a decent salary.

It's the *want* part of money you've got to use as an incentive to get a man to really put out for you. Aim for his heart, aim for what he wants, and you'll always get the best results.

Money is not always a man's prime interest.

As important as money is to all of us, it's not always enough to stimulate a man to do his best for you. You must still concentrate your attention on what he's primarily interested in. I've known men to take a two or three thousand dollar cut in annual salary and leave a place where they weren't treated as gentlemen.

No two men will ever be exactly alike in what it takes to satisfy their individual desires and to make each one of them feel important to himself. You must find out what their individual differences are by your analysis of each one of them.

For example, will Smith be content with a raise in pay alone, or does he want and need a big pat on the back to go along with it? And what about Jones? Does money mean everything to him, or will he be far happier with a letter of appreciation or commendation signed by you?

Oh, don't get me wrong here. I know you can't buy meat and potatoes with a letter of thanks for a job well done, but a word of thanks to your employees will increase their sense of self-importance. It'll pay you dividends in increased sales or production.

4. Always remember a man's name; it's the most important word in all the world to him.

I'm susceptible, too.

My name's important to me, too. It always irritates me when people say, "What was your name again? Was it Van Sneet? Or Van Sleet? Dan Feet?"

During World War II, when I was a young lieutenant with the 44th Division in Eastern France, the Division Commander, General William F. Dean, the same General Dean who later won the Congressional Medal of Honor in the Korean Conflict, called me by name—*Jim*—when he visited the infantry battalion I was with at the front.

I was dumbfounded that a General, my Division Commander, would even know my given name, let alone call me by it. I've never forgotten that small incident. It's one of my brightest memories out of World War II.

5. Motivate a man to feel important to himself by giving him individual identity in your organization.

A man must know why he's there, and he must feel that he belongs where he is.

Everybody has to feel that he belongs somewhere. Each man wants to know that he has his own place in the so-called grand scheme of things. People want to be recognized as belonging to and being identified with some specific group.

Give your employees individual identity as an important member in your organization so you can get each one of them to feel that he really belongs where he is. Show him how he fits into the big picture of your company.

Let him see that he doesn't have just a routine old job with you, but that his is an important role. Let him know that he has a big part to play in the overall effort to get the job done.

Show him that he's both needed and wanted.

You must show a man by your actions that he's both needed and wanted. When a man knows that he's wanted, when he knows that his efforts are sincerely appreciated, when he can feel that he's contributing something toward the achievement of a common goal, then he'll be proud of himself; he'll be proud of those who work with him, and he'll be proud of you and your organization.

So make him feel so proud about his job with you that he'll go down the street saying to everyone, "I work for John Smith, and I wouldn't work for anyone else! Finest man in the world to work for!"

6. A man will feel important to himself, to you and to your organization if you use him primarily in the job for which he's been trained.

Use a man properly.

Not using a man's talents to your best advantage is poor management. You must use the resources of men, money, material, and facilities in the most economical manner possible to accomplish your primary mission. Using a man improperly is the square peg in the round hole idea. So make sure he's working in the job for which he's best fitted, and for which he's been properly trained.

Do this, and, by this one simple act alone, you'll give him a sense of belonging and a feeling of being important to himself, and to you and your organization.

When you put a man on a job without any regard at all for his feelings, his training, or his abilities, you've hurt the man and you've hurt yourself, too. Malassignment is one of the oldest complaints against the military services, but industry is just as guilty. I've seen plenty of examples in both.

A man is much more than a clock-number.

"A man is a name, a person, an individual. He's more than just a clock-number or 'Hey you!'," Jim Richards, the personnel manager for Mid-Western Electric Company in Kansas City, Missouri, told me. "The proper assignment of a man has to start in my department. If I make the initial mistake, it carries right on through into the plant.

"And malassignment of personnel results in dissatisfaction and discontent of the man. But to make it even worse, malassignment causes waste of manpower, resources, time and money. And when we waste all these, we're cutting down on the profits for Mid-Western Electric. And that hurts my pay check, for we work on a salary plus a percentage of the profits basis."

7. Motivate a man to feel important to himself by giving him a personal need and a desire to learn.

Show a man he'll be both recognized and rewarded for his efforts and services.

When you promise a man a reward through higher wages or through a higher position of authority and responsibility, he'll develop and maintain a definite personal interest, not only in his present job, but even more important to you, in his future with your organization.

You must always be sure that you keep your promises. Don't offer a man just empty words and idle lip service. You'll fool him but once with false promises.

You must remember this too. *No amount of motivation will enable a man to do a job that's either too big or too hard for him to do.* When you use a man's talents to your own advantage by assigning him properly, you'll make him important to himself by helping to give him importance and recognition in his job.

Give credit when it's due.

Not only is it important to give credit where it's due; above all, give credit *when it's due.* Make sure you are prompt to encourage early success of a person by giving him the proper recognition and credit for a job well done. Don't wait until tomorrow to compliment a man for a good piece of work that he's done today. The value will be completely lost.

Just like a late birthday card, it fools no one.

Not giving the proper credit when it's due is just about the same as sending someone a late birthday card. You're fooling no one but yourself. It never carries the same message as the one that gets there on time.

The person with the birthday knows that you just forgot all about it. And he also knows that you're not sending it now because you really want to; it's just an afterthought of obligation. Timing is fundamental; it's a must.

8. Give a man a sense of self-importance by keeping him well-informed about his individual progress in your organization.

Insist upon a high state of individual proficiency.

If you insist that a man develop and maintain a high standard of individual proficiency in his work, you'll give him a sense of self-importance in his job. If a man is not well trained in his work, he knows it, and so do his fellow employees.

This alone is enough to shake a man's confidence in the security of his job. If you allow him to get by with slipshod work, he'll question your abilities, too. Whenever a man is afraid of losing his job—whenever his livelihood or his security is threatened in any way—he can't have peace of mind at all. His morale will hit rock-bottom very quickly, and so will the quality of his work.

9. Motivate a man to feel important to himself by rewarding his successes gained through competition with his associates.

Reward success and punish failure.

Competition is a way of throwing down a challenge to your men. Throwing down a challenge is the best way to bring out every last bit of effort from your people. The man who succeeds becomes important, not only to himself, but also to you.

Competition can be used as an incentive to spur your men on to more and greater productive and creative efforts. Such methods may occasionally seem ruthless to you, especially when you have to punish the failures, but competition is the heart and soul of free enterprise. Competition brings progress.

How to punish failure.

Let's talk for a bit about this matter of punishment. The military services use the idea of reward and punishment all the time; parents use it when they discipline their children. It's either licorice or a lickin'. At least, that's what my parents used to offer me.

Teachers use it in school as a way to get the best out of their students and at the same time to keep them under control. Preachers use it more than anyone else when they tell about the glories of Heaven and the fiery torments of Hell.

Your word must be your bond.

"You must always keep your promises to your employees," Tom Powell, manager of Town and Country, a huge discount center in St. Louis, Missouri, told me.

"If you've said you're going to punish a man if he does a certain thing, and then he goes ahead and does it, anyway, being fully aware of the consequences, then you're bound to do what you've said you would do. It always reminds me of the quotation about high prices. *No price is too high if the price is first known!*"

Punishment requires good judgment and a sound sense of justice.

Remember that you'll never motivate a man to do his best for you through constant threats and fear, fear of not meeting production or sales quotas, fear of loss of status, or position, demotion or even dismissal. Fear makes nothing but enemies for you, and it is not a good method of punishment.

To be able to use good judgment and to develop a sound sense of justice, follow these ten guidelines. If you'll keep them always in mind when you're rewarding success or punishing failure, you'll soon develop a reputation for practicing the three F's of motivation: *friendly and fair—but firm.*

(1) *Be fair, prompt, and completely impersonal when you impose punishment.*

Above all, be consistent. Your course must be steady and true, your actions dependable.

And just as a jury should be, when you determine a man's guilt or innocence, you must be completely impersonal and unemotional.

Your heart and sympathy come into the picture when you're deciding what the punishment has to be if the person has been found guilty.

(2) *Consider each individual case on its own merits.*

Always assume that the person is innocent until he's proven guilty beyond a reasonable doubt. Don't convict a man just because he's a Republican and you're a Democrat, or because you're a Protestant and he's a Catholic.

(3) *Always punish in private with dignity and never with a display of anger or temper.*

To remain calm and serene when you're punishing or reprimanding an employee, you should always keep a completely impersonal attitude.

But as I said a moment ago, this doesn't mean that you're not to use understanding, sympathy, and compassion when you do make your decisions as to the kind of punishment or its degree. You're dealing in flesh and blood, you know, not in materials and machinery.

(4) *Check yourself thoroughly to see if you do have or even tend to have any hidden prejudices of any sort.*

If you're prejudiced toward some particular group of people, then you must make a conscious and honest effort to rid yourself of these prejudices. And it'll often be a hard job for you to do. You'll really have to work at it.

Usually, hidden prejudices come from some almost forgotten experience, but the resentment still hangs on. Let's say for example, once your grade school teacher wrapped you over the knuckles with her ruler. But that doesn't give you the right to hate all grade school teachers from that time on, does it?

(5) *If you're prejudiced, then don't let that prejudice enter your decisions.*

If you are prejudiced in some way, and you seem to have a hard time getting rid of those prejudices even when you know they do exist, then at least try to prevent them from creeping into your decisions or influencing your judgment in any way. There's a fairly simple way to tell, that is, if you've got the courage to be completely honest with yourself.

You see, if the punishment you've given in any particular case seems to be beyond what you would normally give, then you have either permitted your prejudice to enter into your decision or you've been completely careless about the whole matter, and you haven't made an honest effort to be just, impartial, and fair in your decision.

(6) *Study and analyze the decisions of others.*

Always study and analyze decisions that have been handed down by those executives who've earned a reputation for being honest, fair, and impartial in their treatment of their employees. History is loaded with examples but so is the present.

(7) *Punish only the guilty person.*

Never use mass punishment. Never punish an entire or even part of a group of employees for the mistakes of one person. You'll only make matters worse if you do.

"This situation will come up when you can't find out who the guilty one is," Captain William Kestner, a basic training company commander at Fort Leonard Wood, Missouri, told me.

"It's often oh-so-tempting to lay down the law to all possible offenders and to punish them all, but it's dynamite if you ever try to control your men this way. It just won't work; so don't try it. Take it from a man who knows!"

(8) *Never play favorites.*

I've touched already on the subject of avoiding cliques. But it's important, for I don't know of a faster or surer way of destroying the morale of your employees than for you to be partial toward a certain person or toward a specific group of persons.

If you favor the incompetent and pass over the deserving, you'll soon find that's all you have left on your hands, the incompetent and the inefficient.

This problem usually comes up when you're trying to play the cloak and dagger game in your plant, and you're using some of your employees for espionage. Leave that game alone. Be an outstanding executive and learn to motivate your employees properly. Then you won't have to play spy.

(9) *Recognize those employees who are worthy of and who've earned the right to receive a commendation or an award.*

Above all, don't become known as the hard-hearted tyrant who dispenses only punishment. Remember that the quality we're discussing here is justice. And justice takes in both punishment and reward, not just punishment alone.

(10) *Always make the person feel that the punishment you're giving him is only a temporary measure.*

Make a man realize and understand that his improvement is not only wanted, that you desire for him to improve, but that you definitely expect him to improve.

The best way to make sure that the punishment is only temporary in the minds of both of you is this: *Once the debt has been paid, forget the incident!*

What kind of punishment?

Well, for example, when a man fails to come to work on time, the time clock penalizes him at once; for when he gets paid, part of his check is missing. That's a built-in automatic punishment.

If he's on a salary basis, instead of punching the time clock in and out, then take some out of his check if he's a continual violator. Just be sure he knows you're going to do it before you do it. No price is too high if the price is first known! Right?

The failure of a man to win a promotion or advancement to a higher position, or his failure to get that raise in salary are punishments in themselves. Or if you didn't give him that letter of appreciation or commendation he expected from you, that becomes a punishment too. Not saying thanks or not giving a man a pat on the back is a punishment to most of us.

You don't have to hit a man with your fist or beat him with a club to punish him, you know. You can be more subtle than that, I'm sure.

Have a reasonable system for promotion and advancement.

Individual progress is morale raising for everyone. If your men know that advancement to a higher position is both possible and probable, this alone will be an important factor in keeping morale at a high level and spurring your men to greater achievements. So you must be sure to have a reasonable system that will present opportunities for promotion and advancement.

The man who's reached his peak can be a problem.

If a man has reached *his* peak, and he knows it—if further advancement and promotion are impossible for him—he'll become stale, and he'll start the down-hill slide from then on.

When a person has reached *his* top, regardless of his age, or his length of time with the organization, there's no other way for him to go but down or out.

10. Make a man feel important to himself by asking for his advice and help.

What's your opinion?

If you want to add to a man's feeling of self-importance, simply ask him for his advice and help. Those few words, *"What's your opinion?"* will send your janitor home bragging to his wife that the president of the corporation had to come to him that day for help in running the show.

Just a word of caution here. When you do ask for a man's

opinion, be courteous enough to hold still and listen to what he has to say. I don't care how fantastic or how outlandish his ideas might sound to you, just listen until he's finished.

And don't disagree with him as soon as he's through. Even though you might know that he's all wrong, don't tell him so. You'll spoil everything if you do. In fact, if you do that, you'd be better off not to ask him for his opinion in the first place.

Listen to him carefully and courteously and then thank him for his opinion, his ideas, and his advice. Tell him that you'll give every possible consideration to his suggestions.

Amazingly enough, if you'll just listen to the ideas of your men, you'll find that they will use their initiative to think up new and better ways of doing things for you which will turn out to be profitable for you. Out of all the chaff you'll have to listen to, you will find some kernels of wheat now and then.

What about a suggestion box?

"I know a lot of companies use the suggestion box system," Paul Mason, the industrial engineering head for King Clothing Corporation in Clayton, Missouri, a suburb of St. Louis, told me. "Of course I'm deeply interested in any suggestions that will improve our efficiency, especially those which suggest improvements in time and motion.

"But to tell the truth, I wouldn't have a suggestion box in the place. They're too impersonal.

"Not only that, a man is never quite sure whether his suggestion is actually read, or just thrown away in the trash at the end of the day, or whenever the box is cleaned out, if it ever is.

"I'd a lot rather listen to a hundred half-baked opinions in person. Sooner or later you're bound to hear some good ideas."

11. Motivate a man to feel self-important by allowing him to set his own goals in his own job.

Emphasize skill—not rules.

Emphasizing skill rather than rules is the way to use mission-type orders. Always judge your subordinates' actions by their results, not upon the way they got those results. As long as the scales of mission and welfare are perfectly balanced, there's no need to concern yourself about how those results were obtained.

Once you can get your men to set their individual goals on their jobs, then you can set your own corporation goals. As the small personal goals are achieved, then the achievement of your corporate goals will follow as a simple matter of course.

12. Let a man develop a sense of importance by showing him how essential his efforts are and where he fits into the big picture.

If a man isn't required in your effort, something's wrong with your organizational set-up.

If you can't explain to every man who works for you how important his job is, why he's there, and how his efforts contribute to the accomplishment of the over-all mission, one of you isn't needed.

Every person who works for you must be thoroughly indoctrinated concerning the importance of his own individual job and its duties, and how it fits into the big picture. A person who feels that he occupies an important spot in your outfit will always be more effective in his work. He'll have a better understanding of why he's there.

It's important that each man understands that a chain is only as strong as its weakest link, and that he's one of the many links in your corporation chain.

Add dignity and stature to his position.

You must add dignity and stature to each man's position in your organization, no matter what that position might be. If you think for one small moment that each man doesn't regard himself as the most important person in the world, you're wrong.

When I went to school, the school janitor was a janitor; today he's a custodial engineer. A street cleaner used to be a street cleaner. Today he's a sanitation worker at the very least, and, in most large cities, he's dignified his position by giving it the title of sanitation engineer.

A farmer is no longer a farmer; he's an agriculturist. He no longer lives on a farm; he has a country place. In a small cafe a cook is a cook; in a big restaurant or hotel he's a chef. And I just read recently that garbage collectors will no longer be known as garbage collectors in a small community in Massachusetts—they're now known as *garbologists.*

13. You can make every man feel important to himself if you'll just put PERSONAL into PERSONNEL!

Always spell PERSONNEL with an AL!

This is where we put the frosting on the cake. But why not? It doesn't cost a penny more to do it. It costs no more to go first class, and you meet much nicer people. All you have to do is add that last little bit of effort to make every single person feel more important to himself!

If you want to be sure you've spelled PERSONNEL with an AL, if you want to make sure you've put the PERSONAL into your PERSONNEL relations, ask yourself these questions each time you finish a *human-relations-transaction:*

(1) *Have you treated the other person as you'd like to be treated yourself?*

Did you treat him as a fellow human being? Did the color of his skin, his politics, or his religion influence your judgement? If it did, you shouldn't have hired that man in the first place.

(2) *Did you handle every piece of paper with a name on it as a person—or just another piece of paper?*

(3) *Did you weigh each case on its individual merits?*

Did you consider the welfare of that man, the welfare of the rest of the men, and the mission of the entire organization when you made your decision?

(4) *Did you answer all the questions that were raised, or did you leave the person in doubt about some of the answers?*

Did you look up the answers for him, or was that just too much trouble for you? Did you promise him an answer later on? And did you fulfill that promise, your solemn obligation to him?

(5) *When you were in doubt did you seek the advice of others?*

Did you try to bluff your way through? Did you try to guess and make believe that you knew it all, or did you ask for the help of some older and wiser heads than yours?

(6) *When you gave your answer, were you justly proud of the understanding and the tolerance you showed in your decision?*

Did you use the human touch, or did you just give the man the bum's rush to get him out of your office?

(7) *Did you tell the person why you couldn't go along with his request, if you honestly couldn't?*

Did you tell him why you had to say "No," or was that too much trouble and inconvenience for you?

(8) *Are you truly proud of what you said to the man and how you said it?*

What would have been your reaction to the language you used in your reply if you'd been on the receiving end? If you had it to do all over again, would your answer have been the same?

To Sum It All Up

Make a man important *to himself.* Give a man importance. Help him to build his self-esteem. Lend dignity and respect to his job. Do that, and you'll motivate him to do what you want him to do even if the first ten dynamic laws of motivation fail to persuade and move him.

If you'll make a man and his work important to himself, if you're hearty in your approbation and lavish in your praise of him, he'll want to do what you want him to do.

But if you try to push him to do something against his will, you'll never get the job done. Remember that *the head never hears 'till the heart has listened.* You'll motivate a man by winning his heart—not his head!

Recapitulation of the Thirteen Keys for Application of the Eleventh Dynamic Law of Motivation

1. *You'll motivate a man to feel important to himself when you appeal to his heart and not his head!*
2. *Motivate a man to feel important to himself by becoming genuinely interested in him and in what he does.*
3. *Make a man feel important to himself by talking in terms of his interests.*
4. *Always remember a man's name; it's the most important word in all the world to him.*
5. *Motivate a man to feel important to himself by giving him individual identity in your organization.*
6. *A man will feel important to himself, to you and to your organization if you use him primarily in the job for which he's been trained.*
7. *Motivate a man to feel important to himself by giving him a personal need and a desire to learn.*
8. *Give a man a sense of self-importance by keeping him well-informed about his individual progress in your organization.*
9. *Motivate a man to feel important to himself by rewarding his successes gained through competition with his associates.*
10. *Make a man feel important to himself by asking for his advice and help.*
11. *Motivate a man to feel self-important by allowing him to set his own goals in his own job.*
12. *Let a man develop a sense of importance by showing him how essential his efforts are and where he fits into the big picture.*
13. *You can make every man feel important to himself if you'll just put PERSONAL into PERSONNEL!*

Dynamic Law #12

Put the First Eleven
Into Action
and Make Them Work!

When—Where—Who—Which One?

To use the right dynamic law of motivation at the right time on the right man, you must have a complete understanding of each one of your employees.

The ability to influence and direct other people, to get them to do what you want them to do—the art of motivation—requires a complete understanding, predicting, and controlling of their behavior.

You'll be able to motivate your men properly to do what you want them to do when you make a constant effort to thoroughly understand them. When you do have a complete understanding of each employee and what really makes him tick, then you'll be able to know which dynamic law of motivation to use on which man, and when and where to use it!

When you realize that no two men will respond exactly alike to your actions and orders, you'll soon learn which dynamic law of motivation will best motivate each one of them to do his best for you.

206

Each one of your actions and orders will have a different effect on each one of your men. When you learn how each one of them will respond differently and what that response is going to be you'll know which dynamic law of motivation to apply so you can properly motivate that individual to do exactly what you want him to do.

Understanding each individual will help you to mold the entire group into an effective team.

The individual reactions of all your employees will be molded into a group attitude toward you and the work assigned by you. If you can get desirable reactions from the individual employees in your organization, you can also expect to get a favorable group reaction. This favorable group reaction will allow you to control all your employees as one big effective team.

Why the Dynamic Laws of Motivation Work for You

Once a minister said to me, "If it weren't for the people in the church, the church would be a wonderful thing!" I'm afraid he'd lost sight of the basic mission of the church. We might as well accept the facts. People are everything! If you didn't have people to work with, there'd be no use for the dynamic laws of motivation. If that minister didn't have people to preach to, there'd be no use for a church, would there? We can't operate in a vacuum.

The dynamic motivation of people is largely a matter of knowing, predicting, and controlling their behavior and their actions. When you can control a person's behavior you'll automatically be able to control his actions and reactions.

But again, you'll be able to do that only if you make an earnest effort to understand him. You don't have to be a psychologist or have a college degree to figure other people out, but you'll never get the best results from your employees unless you really understand why they do what they do.

Everything that you and I do in life is based upon our fulfillment of certain basic needs and wants that we have. Our efforts to get what we want out of life bring about what psychologists like to call *human behavior patterns.*

But if you can always remember to use the following thought in the motivation of your employees and everything you do is directed toward helping them achieve the goals I'm going to give you, you'll never have the slightest bit of trouble in motivating them to do what you want them to do. In fact, you'll soon have the psychologists and the psychiatrists coming to you for help. Just remember this thought and apply it.

Every normal person wants to know how to be loved, how to win money, fame and fortune, power, and how to stay healthy.

If you'll help every one of your employees from the lowest-paid janitor to your highest-paid executive to get these goals of his by properly applying the correct dynamic law of motivation at the right place at the right time, you, too, will be able to achieve success in life. *By helping them achieve their goals, you'll automatically obtain your own. You'll be able to get what you want out of life for yourself.*

The Three Basic Elements Which Affect the Dynamic Laws of Motivation the Situation—the Motivated—the Motivator

"Motivation of my employees is affected by three basic elements," Charles Crane, president of Crane Plumbing and Heating, St. Louis, Missouri, told me. "Those three elements are the motivator, the motivated, and the situation in which they both operate or work. In short, motivation of them is affected by me and my other executive assistants—by them—and by what we're doing that day."

In short, Mr. Crane is saying this: There's no standard recipe for making an executive, and no two executives ever get results in exactly the same way. In fact, no two of them will apply the dynamic laws of motivation in precisely the same way, and yet both of them will get results when they use them.

But each executive or motivator of others in analyzing the various parts of a problem in motivation, will be affected in a different way by the influence of his own personality, the personalities of the people who work for him, and the factors of the situation which he faces.

All these variances make impossible the use of a template or a standardized solution. But any reasonably intelligent person, no matter how inexperienced he might be in the beginning, can study, practice, cultivate, apply, and finally perfect his own techniques in the application of the dynamic laws of motivation.

The situation.

No two situations are exactly alike.

Nothing is so constant in this world as change. Each situation must be faced as a new and separate problem, no matter how much it looks like something you've seen in the past. It might be close to what you've seen before, but it won't be identical. Each problem must have its own answer, and you'll have to make a constant evaluation of the situation as it changes.

The various situations and problems which will arise to confront you each day will require your full abilities as a manager, an executive, a motivator.

The motivated.

Your actions and orders.

You must realize that your actions and orders will have a different effect on each one of your men, and that each one of them will respond differently. The resulting interplay of all these reactions among individuals of the group will end up in a definite group attitude toward you and toward any task you assign to them.

If you can get desirable reactions from the individual employees in your organization, you can also expect to get a desirable group reaction. Then you'll be able to mold this group of individuals into an effective working team.

Your contacts with them.

"My biggest problem is communication," says Reed Dawson, a plant manager for Allied Industries, Inc. "You see, as plant manager, I'm in close personal contact with only a relatively small group even though we employ nearly 1,400 people here in Springfield alone. I couldn't possibly make my desires known to each one of my employees, so I have to depend upon that small group to make my will known and to execute my purposes."

It's so true. The success of an organization will depend upon the top executive's ability to promote effective relationships between himself, the group, and the individual members of that group. You must promote such a healthy atmosphere of cooperation that your subordinates will work together with mutual respect and confidence.

The Six Factors That Shape a Man's Personality

All people are different in varying degrees from each other. Each man's personality is the dynamic product of all his heredity, environment, and experiences, as well as the interaction of all his physical, mental, and emotional characteristics. And these characteristics will vary from person to person.

1. Heredity.

Heredity is the name we give to the general statement that offspring closely resemble their parents. Such a broad statement is based on the observed facts of life and science. It's that transmission of certain physical and mental characteristics of parents to their children.

Your child might be another Einstein or president or . . .

Your child might, for example, inherit all the potential intelligence and all the possible qualifications to become a great scientist, a brilliant composer or musician, a painter, a poet.

He could inherit the physical potential to become a professional football player, a basketball or baseball star. All these inherited characteristics don't always have to come straight from the parents either. Sometimes they seem to skip a generation or so. Then you have to look back at the grandparents or even the great grandparents to find out where these certain physical or mental traits came from.

In my own case, for example.

In my own case, I'm only five and a half feet tall. Two of my children are already taller than I am by at least 3 to 4 inches. But their great grandparents on both sides of the family were tall. Of course, environment can influence that growth, too, as you'll see in just a moment or so when we take it up.

You inherit only the potential.

To inherit the potential for greatness doesn't mean that it's going to be developed automatically. The attainment of that inherited potential will depend a great deal upon the person's environment and his experiences.

You see, a child can inherit only the potential and not the real thing. Your son could inherit all the potential to become a great concert pianist, but unless his environment offers him the chance to develop this inherited talent, well, it's all going to go to waste, isn't it?

2. Environment.

Environment is the sum total.

Environment is the sum total of all the conditions, the influences, and the forces around us that will change and modify our lives and the development of our hereditary potential.

Our environment takes in such things as the influence of our parents, our brothers and our sisters, our friends. The kind of church we go to when we're young can affect our future growth as responsible citizens. The schools we attend also have a great influence upon our future development.

The kind of community we grow up in, the kind of books we read, the television programs we watch, the kinds of hobbies we have, even the food we eat, all these will be influencing factors in our environment.

Take food for instance.

The third and fourth generations of American Japanese who live here in these United States are five to six inches taller and many pounds heavier than their great grandparents who came to this country from Japan.

I'm not referring to those who've increased in height and weight because of intermarriages with Caucasians either. I mean those who still remain pure Japanese in their blood lines, but who were born here in the United States and who are American citizens by birth.

"Our increases in height and weight are thought to be due primarily to better food and to better living conditions," Paul Miyamoto, a Los Angeles friend of mine said. "I'm nearly 40 pounds heavier than my father and I'm just short of 6 feet while he was barely 5 feet 3.

"I guess this seems to show that beef and wheat eaters grow bigger and stronger, and maybe even live longer, than do rice and fish eaters."

This is only one example of how environment can change and influence your life. There's no limit to the examples of environmental influence we could pursue. But that's a subject which deserves separate study, and our time is far too limited for that. So let me sum it all up for you this way.

The environmental conditions will either speed up or slow down the development of the inherited mental and physical potential of a person. And that's it in a nutshell.

3. Experience.

Experience is everything that's ever happened to you.

Experience is the actual living through of an event. It's everything that's ever happened to you. It includes everything you've ever heard or seen or done. It plays a powerful and influential part in your emotional growth in that final shaping of your basic attitudes and prejudices. Unfortunately, these attitudes and prejudices show through too easily in our overall personalities as expressed in our actions.

No two of us can possibly be alike.

The differences in heredity, environment, and experience will cause some of the differences in us. No two of us can possibly be exactly alike. Each one of us is the result of his own peculiar heredity, his own environment, and his own experiences. So our viewpoint of how to get our basic needs and wants are all completely different, one from another.

If this weren't already enough to confuse and complicate our understanding of each other, to add to the difficulty, we need to look at a person's physical, mental, and emotional traits. Then the variety of possibilities in people and their differences from each other goes nearly beyond the capability of comprehension.

4. Physical and (5) mental characteristics.

The kind of work you're best fitted for . . .

The kind of work that each one of us is best suited for will be greatly influenced by our physical and our mental abilities. These particular characteristics will help to determine the kinds of physical work and mental activity each one of us likes to do best.

Some people seem to be naturally gifted with an inborn knack of being more adept at an occupation that requires the use of their hands or the kind of work that takes a manual skill and a certain dexterity. Personally, I can't hammer a nail straight. When my wife sees me with a hammer and a nail in my hand, she covers her ears and heads for the bedroom and shuts the door.

Other people seem better equipped by nature to perform complex and intricate mental tasks that require the use of reason and deduction.

Why malassignment brings trouble.

If a person is given a job to do that lies beyond his mental or his physical capabilities, he'll at once become discouraged and frustrated. He'll end up with a feeling of resentment and hatred toward the person who gave him the job to do in the first place.

And by the same token, if a bright person is given a dull and monotonous piece of work to do, he'll be insulted. He'll react in exactly the same way with exactly the same end results.

The person who's been given work to do that's not what he can best do is not being properly used. We say that he's been malassigned. Remember, that's a big word used today in personnel management which simply means you've put a square peg in the round hole.

But at any rate, you can't expect a man to give his utmost either as an individual or to the combined efforts of the group if he's not properly assigned to a job he can best do for you.

6. Emotional characteristics.

The head never hears 'til the heart has listened.

Your emotional characteristics are extremely important in deciding what your final personality is going to be like. If we had some way to scientifically measure emotion objectively and accurately, we'd find that it's the over-riding factor in our personalities and in our actions.

That's why we always say that the head never hears 'til the heart has listened. Emotion often drives us to do the things we know are not quite the best for us to do. I suppose that's why some of us smoke too much, some of us drink too much, some of us become dope addicts, and on and on.

I'm reminded of the Army sergeant who said to me, "I've been through Tokyo six times and I haven't actually seen the city yet. But oh—h—those beautiful Japanese girls!"

Unfortunately, when we make decisions, emotion often rules over reason, common sense, good judgment, and past experience. It's the most unreliable and the most unpredictable part of our personalities.

And it's also the hardest area to understand in your efforts to control and motivate your employees. But you must understand how and why people react emotionally the way they do when they face difficult problems, frustration, criticism, and even hardship or danger.

Under pressure, one man may become extremely angry, another may quit and walk out on you, yet another might react calmly or perhaps with a quiet resignation to the facts of the situation. The important thing is this. You must know which man is going to do which thing!

There's no doubt about it. Emotional actions and reactions will give you your most difficult problems to solve in this field of human behavior, human relations, and motivation of others to do what you want them to do.

We're all alike in one respect however.

Although none of us are exactly alike in our physical, our mental and emotional makeups, we are all much alike in one respect, and that's in the effort we make to fulfill our basic needs and wants.

So. From a motivation point of view, we have no further interest in these six elements of human nature except as they influence a person's actions and reactions in his attempts to get what he wants out of life. Any further study of them from any other point of view would be a complete waste of our time, at least, as far as the dynamics of motivation is concerned.

The real important point to remember about people is this. Just learn how each one of these six facets of a person's personality affects the fact that *he wants to know how to be loved, how to win money, fame or fortune, power, and how to stay healthy.*

Once you've learned that for each person whom you motivate, you'll be a lot further along the path to the understanding of human nature and human behavior than the average student of psychology ever will be.

The Basic Eight

We can break a person's needs and wants down into 8 specifics. There are what those psychologists say each one of us strives for. I choose to call them *the basic eight.*

At any rate, every normal person wants these things out of life:

1. Health and the preservation of life.
2. Food and drink.
3. Sleep.
4. Love.
5. Money and the things money will buy.
6. The well-being of our loved ones.
7. Life in the hereafter.
8. A feeling of importance.

Their order or importance.

I haven't listed these eight needs and wants in any certain order of any particular importance. Aside from certain purely physical body needs such as food, drink, and sleep, the order of precedence depends entirely upon your own individual viewpoint.

You'll also find that the order of importance can shift up and down the scale daily, even hourly. But no matter in what order you put these needs and wants, *everything that you do in life is directed toward your getting them. And so are the efforts of every one of your employees too!*

Is it a need or a want?

Sometimes it's hard to tell distinctly whether a certain objective is a need or a want. Many times one certain thing is a need up to a certain point, but beyond that it becomes purely a want, a desire.

For example, you could list hamburger as a need; porterhouse steak becomes a want. Bread is the poor man's protein; meat, the rich man's. A house with one bathroom could be thought of as a basic need; one with three bathrooms becomes a want. Heat in the winter is a necessity; a fireplace for most of us is a convenience. A woman's cloth coat in winter is a need; a mink stole is a want.

Are there variations of these?

I've listed here what I consider as *the basic eight*. I suppose you could name some variations of them, but I think when you're through, you'll still be able to jell them all down into these eight basic wants and needs I've given you.

But for instance, physical comfort could be considered as a part of health; social approval and the satisfaction of one's ego could be included as a part of the desire for a feeling of importance.

Security depends upon you.

Security could be implied in more than one way, I suppose. Some people might think of security as being only money and the things money will buy; others might feel that security is better defined in terms of life in the hereafter.

Still others could feel they have security in the love of their wives and children. But as I've said, I think you can add and subtract—multiply and divide—interpret all you want to, but when you're all through, you'll still wind up with these basic eight.

Happiness is . . .

Happiness is many things to many people. You might not be satisfied with anything less than the best stereo equipment that money can buy; I might be tone deaf and not enjoy music at all. I might want a library full of the best books; you might not care to read as your way of relaxation. (But I hope you do!) I could enjoy eating Oriental foods; you might despise them.

But happiness is a relative matter anyway, just as how much we want of something is relative. The primary value of a Cadillac is only if your neighbor happens to own a Chevrolet.

But enough about the motivated. Now let's turn to the most important subject of all—the Motivator—You!

The Motivator—You!

Executives are made, not born!

The United States is one country where the majority of people believe, and that belief has been proven by thousands, that any one, with the proper application of effort, can rise above the level of his birth.

Many officers in the armed services start as enlisted men; in fact, most of them do. Corporation presidents have started as office boys; people still become millionaires today in spite of high taxes. It can be done.

Many studies have been conducted hoping to cover some single magic trait which could be pinned down as the key factor to a person's success. But the many lists of personal qualities proposed by authorities in this field showed many differences of opinion.

All good leaders, all outstanding executives and top-level managers, all have had some of the required qualities. None have had all of them. Very few have had identical strong points. One fact did come out of all these studies. And that is that successful people succeed in spite of their weaknesses. However, it's best to emphasize your good points.

The wise executive capitalizes on his strong points.

The good executive must constantly evaluate himself to determine which personal qualities will best help him in gaining the willing obedience, confidence and respect, loyal cooperation and full support from all his men.

And it's important that you make an honest self-evaluation to determine the degree to which you possess the desirable characteristics of a leader, such traits as bearing, courage, integrity, dependability, and all the rest we've discussed as we've come along.

After you determine your best points, not only should you improve on them, *you must capitalize on them.* At the same time, take positive steps to improve your weak traits.

Of course, some great names have even taken their weak points and emphasized them until they've become their strongest features. Take Jimmy Durante and his nose, for example. Bob Hope and his ski nose; Dean Martin and his booze. I'm not quite sure how you'd classify General MacArthur's pride or General Patton's temper.

Your actions and orders.

Your actions and your orders are the techniques you'll use to initiate the courses of action you think best for the accomplishment of your many responsibilities.

Because of the many factors involved, you cannot be completely certain that any action you take or any order you give will be completely successful. Communication, the transmission of your desires to the lowest working level, is one of the biggest problems you'll have to solve in a big corporation.

However, you can predetermine the soundness and logic of any order or any proposed action by examining your techniques to see if they follow these three guidelines:

1. The order should accomplish or aid in the accomplishment of one or both of the two main basic responsibilities—to accomplish the mission—consider the welfare.

2. The order must always be guided by the dynamic laws of motivation.

3. The order must take advantage of your strong personality traits.

Your supervision.

A top-notch executive will usually find that he'll spend much more time in the supervision of the action that is under way than he will in the formulation and issuance of new actions and orders to be performed.

To supervise properly, you must develop sufficient proficiency in the area you're checking to be sure that you can recognize when the work is not going satisfactorily.

You must be able to supervise in such a way that the work can be checked without undue harassment of your employees.

Your evaluation.

A military leader evaluates his unit continually in the light of the four indicators of military leadership: morale, esprit de corps, discipline, and individual proficiency. Even if you use these four, or some of them, you must add at least one or two more to your check-list. *Profit and progress.*

Profit for today is expressed in terms of dividends for stockholders. Progress for tomorrow is expressed in terms of growth and expansion for the future. Both of these are your responsibilities whether you're the corporation president or a production supervisor.

In summary then . . .

In the final analysis, motivation is the presentation of an opportunity to a man in such a way that it will allow him to get what he wants, but in such a way that his getting it will simultaneously allow you to get what you want.

The fact that you get what you want, as a result of his getting what he wants, must appear to be pure coincidence if not by sheer accident. To best furnish this opportunity to each one of your men, use the dynamic laws of motivation which are:

1. *You've got to know your business—and stick to it!*
2. *If you want to improve—be honest with yourself.*
3. *Know your men and look out for their welfare.*
4. *Always keep your men informed.*
5. *Make sure the task is understood, supervised, and accomplished.*
6. *Train your men as a team.*
7. *Make sound and timely decisions.*
8. *Develop a sense of responsibility in your subordinates.*
9. *Seek responsibility and take responsibility for your actions.*
10. *Always set the example.*
11. *Motivate every single man to feel important to himself.*
12. *Put the first eleven into action and make them work!*

Only 5 make the grade!

Out of every 100 people, 95 become followers. Only 5 become leaders. Out of every 100 people, 95 percent fail. Only 5 percent succeed.

May you be one of the 5 percent!